STARING
INTO WATER

PETER FOSTER

Time is an Ocean Publications

Time is an Ocean Publications
An Imprint of **write***ahead*
Lonsdale Road
Wolverhampton WV3 0DY

First Printed Edition published
by **Time is an Ocean Publications 2021**
Text copyright ©**Peter Foster**
Copyright of all photographs are ascribed individually at the
back of the book
Front and back cover pictures ©**Peter Foster**
The right of **Peter Foster** to be identified as the author of
this work has been asserted by him, in accordance with the
Copyright, Designs and Patents Act 1988.

DEDICATION

This book is dedicated to the two women who
had a great impact on my life.
The first, **Miss Mary Weatherall** - one of
Yorkshire's finest educators - set me off on the
right path to live a fruitful and respectful life.
The second, **Edwina** became my eternal partner,
my long-suffering wife and best friend.
She kept me on that path and never let me go to
work in a dirty shirt.

Contents

Foreword

Coming from a good working class family, Peter's early childhood saw him sailing the oceans, cruising down the Suez Canal and settling with his family for almost four years in Aden, South Yemen.

Going to school with nuns as his teachers, Peter grasped the way of life in an Arab country in quick time. He soon found that he and his siblings were pretty much left to their own devices as their parents enjoyed a never-ending round of socialising and as this parental behaviour gathered pace, the seeds of destruction were gradually being sown in plain sight right under Peter's very nose.

With his father suffering a catastrophic illness that required urgent medical attention back in the UK, the family headed home after almost four years in the Red Sea paradise.

With Aden consigned to memory, life back in England started off okay, but Peter's father was becoming more and more dependent on alcohol and was the prime cause of his mother's suicide in January 1965.

The family was ripped apart overnight. Peter's world exploded into a thousand pieces, his maternal grandmother wanted nothing to do with him or his father. With his siblings scattered, Peter and his father were on their own.

Going from rented flats to lodgings, they soon left a trail of moonlight flits behind them eventually living and sleeping in his father's car.

Driving the length of the country from Yorkshire to Devon, Peter met his aunt, uncle and cousins for the first time in many years. Peter's father then deserted him, leaving him in their care.

This was the start of a nightmare. Beatings, isolation and ridicule were served up in equal portions during Peter's stay of almost seven months.

Reunited with his father, he then spent three months living in the car as they made their way from Devon back to Yorkshire. Peter's father was sinking deeper into alcoholism, at times floundering. The squalid state and atmosphere of the car was made even worse by his father's incontinence.

Fate stepped in after three months on the road when Peter was suddenly taken into care.

The children's home in West Yorkshire where he was sent, was to some extent a welcome relief, with regular food, clean clothes and a warm bed. But life in the home was hard with no love nor compassion shown to the boys who were forced to live there.

Memories of those days are burned deep into Peter's consciousness. With a sharp mind, the incidents are as fresh to him now as the day they occurred.

These memories and more are firmly etched clearly as Peter commits to paper his first-hand account of four traumatic years in his life on the road and ultimately in a bleak children's home during the mid-1960s.

Chapter One

Paradise in the Sun

Passage to Aden on the SS Nevasa

I heard the clock in the hallway strike 2am. The start of a new year. New hopes and new aspirations for the celebrating partygoers out that night to ring out the old and ring in the new.

For me, a 12-year-old lad without a care in the world, the dawning of 1st January 1965 was about to rip my world apart and catapult me headlong into a downward spiral of moral decay, bullying and abuse. It was the day my world changed dramatically for the worst.

It wasn't always that way. With the love of good parents, coupled with a father who was an excellent provider, I and my siblings, Kathleen, Susan and David, had enjoyed what could be termed an enviable life up to that point. David was six years my senior, a tall good-looking lad with dark brown wavy hair and a pop star appearance. Some would say he was the spitting image of pop idol Billy Fury. I worshipped the ground he trod on.

At the time, David was away in the Royal Navy. When he came home on leave, it was the best of times for me. I would get off the school bus and run the three quarters of a mile from the bus stop to the bottom of our drive. From the road-end up to our house, the *Lodge*, the distance was about three hundred yards. David would hang his sailor cap in the front room window, easily seen from the main road, the white circular cap was unmistakable, and it was our signal. I would run up the drive with ever quickening steps to see my big brother.

We would often practise unarmed combat on the front lawn, rolling about having a terrific time. I remember once I managed to get him down on the ground for a submission. Happy days those were. David was my half-brother and Kathleen my half-sister; both children of my mother and her first husband. Susan was also my half-sister, a child of my father's first marriage. I was the only issue from the union of my mother and father. I had no full blood relations with my siblings. But that did not seem to matter back then.

Susan was working away from home in a hotel. We didn't see too much of her and she seemed to prefer it that way. For me, it was Kathleen who I was closest to. We had never been separated and she was always a constant influence in my life. She was five years older than me and I guess she was the one who I would turn to for advice.

But since our return from Aden, our parents were always arguing. My mother would retreat to the bedroom and would spend days in bed leaving Kath to make the meals and do the housework. This was pretty much the way of things since my father had come out of hospital after almost dying from a ruptured ulcer while we were abroad.

Kath was my rock; she was a bouncy girl and would always include me in what she was doing. A slim lass with shoulder length brown hair with a gentle undulating wave running through it and freckles all over her face.

I remember once going into the bathroom. There she was, lying in the bath fully clothed reading a magazine.

"I've not gone crazy," she said, not bothering to look up, *"I'm just shrinking me new jeans."* Apparently, it was a thing. If you put a pair of new jeans on and sat in a bath of water for long enough, they would shrink to fit you like a glove. Can't honestly say that it worked for my sister.

Working for the government in the Civil Service, my father was an exceptionally intelligent and talented aero/electrical designer.

Early in 1959, such were his talents that he secured a dream posting to Aden, South Yemen with a brief to help design and oversee the electrical installations and development of the new oil refinery being built in partnership with the United States.

My mother, brother, sisters and I followed six months later by sea. We left Southampton on the SS Nevasa. It was a newly commissioned troopship, the first to be launched since the Second World War on the Clyde in 1955. She plied her trade carrying troops, families and cargo mainly down through the Red Sea and into the Indian Ocean and on to places such as Singapore and Thailand. The SS Nevasa was converted into a school ship in the early 1960s and became a useful tool for educational cruises. But after a life at sea of just 20 years, she was scrapped in 1975.

A fabulous time lay ahead as we settled into cruise life for the next three to four weeks. The trip out of the English Channel was uneventful but pleasant.

"Just wait until we reach the Bay of Biscay," said Ernest, our cabin steward. He went on, *"You'll need to make sure you hold on tight when we get there, and best stay off the deck as well."*

Ernest's prediction came alarmingly true. The ship rolled and pitched, deck chairs slid down the deck, plates and cutlery rattled in the dining room and more than one person was seen to be suffering the effects of the dreaded *mal de mer…* myself included. I spent all day in my bed clutching a wastepaper basket thinking my whole world was coming to an end.

When we eventually reached the Mediterranean Sea, life was a totally different affair. The sea was so blue. I had never seen it that colour before. Every time we had been to Blackpool, the sea looked grey and dark, almost like liquid mud at times and very uninviting. By this time, we were also feeling the benefit of the much warmer climate the Mediterranean had to offer.

Reaching Port Said, we entered the Suez Canal, and what an experience it was for a seven-year-old. Proceeding at a sedentary pace through the canal, we could now see life on both banks of the waterway. Arab children were running up and down shouting and waving at us, cattle with humps on their backs pulling carts and then there were the camels. I had never seen so many camels before, some being ridden, some were pulling big carts and some just ambling around.

Their big floppy lips were the source of much amusement to us kids. My sisters, brother and I couldn't tear ourselves away from the safety railings running around the upper deck of the ship. It was amazing. Going through Great Bitter Lake and the lesser Little Bitter Lake was the best.

There were miles of sand banks rising up out of the water. Here would lie crocodiles, mostly small - around four or five feet long. But every so often, there was a massive one, stretched out, stock still, its huge jaw wide open showing rows and rows of teeth that would be the last thing many a Suez fish saw before sliding down its gullet.

Out of the Suez Canal, through the Gulf of Suez, into the Red Sea.

"Not long to wait now," said Ernest, *"Just a few days and we reach the Indian Ocean and there your father will be, waiting for you in Aden."*

I remember the first time I saw my father after he had left England six months previously to travel on his own to Aden. He was to get himself settled and set up a home for us to follow him at a later date. It was a mixture of happiness tinged with more than a little embarrassment and pain.

By the time we sailed into Steamer Point, the main port and thoroughfare in Aden, we hadn't seen our father for over six months. I was keen to make an impression. That year, 1959, was the age of the teddy boys and slicked back, greasy hair was all the rage. I helped myself to a great dollop of Brylcreem, lathering it all over my head before going up on deck to see if my father was waiting at the dock side for us.

He was, and so was the relentless sun, beating down mercilessly on everyone and everything. We had the luxury of air conditioning on the ship so it wasn't as noticeable but now, on the dock side, with the white hull of the ship reflecting every single ray, it was unbearable.

Worse still, my Brylcreem started to melt! Down my face. Into my eyes. Into my mouth. It was everywhere. I could taste it and my eyes were stinging.

My father thought it was hilarious, *"You'll soon get used to the heat,"* he laughed.

Our first apartment was across the street from the cattle sheds in Crater. That first night in Aden was interesting to say the least. The flat was also home to several families of lizards. Geckos they were called; they could walk up walls and across ceilings as easily as I could walk on the pavement.

I had two sharing my bedroom. I couldn't take my eyes off them and I dared not drop off to sleep. David, terrific big brother that he was, told me that if I went to sleep, they would come down and crawl all over my head and face.

Not much sleep for me that night, but to be fair I was so excited. The geckos were a secondary thought and I soon grew to live with them and give them names. My first attempt to catch one was an experience I can still re-live to this day. They were quick and when I tried to grab the largest - I had named him *Bluey* due to his colour - its tail came off in my hand! I learned later that this was a built-in defence mechanism, and the gecko wasn't harmed and would regenerate a new one in a short time. *Bluey* was awarded a name change - *Stumpy* seemed more appropriate from that time on.

Crater was a township built inside the rim of an extinct volcano. The smell wasn't exactly pleasant due to our location in the vicinity of the cattle shed but with everything around us a totally new experience, it didn't seem to matter.

Just after we arrived, I was struck down with some sort of tropical disease that put me in the local hospital for several weeks.

We had explicit instructions from our father to only drink water that had first been boiled and then put in the fridge. For a seven-year-old, water straight out of the tap looked the same and it was very much easier to get.

Herein lay my downfall. After drinking the tap water for the duration of the first week or so my body exploded in boils and blisters. They were in my hair, covering my head and all over my face and body. The pain was excruciating particularly whenever one of the boils was getting ripe for squeezing.

It all came to a head one afternoon when I came up behind my sister Kathleen with a brush. It wasn't one of those brushes with a long handle and a brush head that we are so familiar with in the UK.

This was more a bundle of long grasses tapered to a solid base and bound tight to form the handle. I swished it across the back of Kath's legs, but the response wasn't what I was expecting as it was clear I had surprised her.

She whipped round in an instant and at the same time caught me across the face with her flailing hand. Boils and pimples erupted in a mixture of puss and blood. I passed out and only started to come round on the way to the hospital.

My memory of the next few days in hospital is very vague. My sister's actions had caused some sort of reaction within my body and I was floating in and out of consciousness.

When it came for me to be up and about, I only then learned that I had been seriously ill. It was a good thing that I went to the hospital as the boils and blisters were just a side effect of the disease, there was something much more sinister going on.

For the next three weeks, I underwent treatment; blisters were popped, boils were lanced and blood was infused. I began to look like an Egyptian mummy with all the bandages around my body. I had a raging fever that caused a few days of my hospital visit to be permanently erased from my memory.

For obvious reasons, not being allowed out of the hospital was distressing for all of us. I would will the clock to move around so that visiting time would come quicker.

Each day was like this until I was fully recovered and eventually allowed to go back home.

Off to school in sun drenched Aden

I, nor anyone else at the time, didn't realise or know that this incident in hospital would come back to haunt me years later, in my late 30s, in the form of heart disease.

The following years flew by in a blur of sun, sea, swimming and fishing… it was a great time for any youngster. The average day would see me at school for a 7.30am start and a 12.30pm finish. It was just too hot in the afternoons for schooling.

My school, St Joseph's School for Boys, was exactly what it said on the tin - no girls at all. The only females were the teachers, the nuns. One nun in particular was a fearsome lady whose reputation reached my ears from my peers before I had the pleasure of meeting her. She was a big lady, easily six feet tall and with, I guess, underneath her gowns, a body to match. A real powerhouse of a woman. Sister Clara towered over me.

The sight I witnessed when I met her was intimidating - a long black gown all the way up to her neck gave way to a white cowl across her shoulders that continued up to cover her entire head, leaving just her face framed in white. Her head was covered by a black cloth that flowed down her back. This woman commanded respect. I made up my mind there and then to be an exemplary student.

Sister Clara's skin was much darker than the other teachers and her accent, although perfectly understandable in English, was also different. She also possessed a superpower, an uncanny ability to hit any chosen pupil irrespective of where they were sitting with the blackboard rubber. I once suffered the ignominy of the rubber on the side of my head. My ear was still ringing when I was on my way home.

When she wasn't at the blackboard and we were writing at our desks, Sister Clara would walk up and down the aisle between the desks very slowly, looking at our work as she passed by. In her hand was an extremely long and supple plastic ruler. It was always one or the other in her hand; the blackboard rubber or the ruler. If she spotted a mistake, wham! With a flick of the wrist, the ruler would flick out and land on the back of your hand with a loud smack. No one had to look up and around the room to know Sister Clara had struck again. This lady was so deserving of her reputation.

Those early days in my school life were difficult. The nuns taught predominantly in Arabic. But it didn't take long for me to fit in. I was soon writing in Arabic, and backwards at that!

The flat in Crater wasn't far from the sea. Whenever I could find the slightest excuse, I would be off to spend every spare moment down at the small but busy fishing harbour. I remember the walk down; camel carts were everywhere and by now I didn't give them a second look. Excrement in the streets, human at that, was everywhere.

There was some sort of beach area to the right as I rounded the bend and saw the sea, but no sand, just piles of scarified rubble. This is where the small, homemade boats, almost like one-man canoes were scattered around.

The Arabs would take their boats out and fish with a handline over the side. Those little craft didn't look to be very safe when they took to the water. They wobbled almost to the point of tipping over. Every day, the fishermen would all return at pretty much the same time and I would always make sure I was down there to watch.

Every kind of fish came ashore, eels, sharks, ray, parrot fish, angel fish, the list of species and the colours were endless. Most of the catch would be sold right there and then, straight out of the canoe. It was surprising how many Europeans, friends of my parents, would gather to buy the fresh fish.

It wasn't a case of how much please? The fishermen would take advantage of this type of approach and charge an exorbitant price. The way it was done was by bartering. The fishermen would start the process: *"Five shilling?"*

"No, I'll give you one shilling."

"Four shilling?"

"No, One shilling."

"Three shilling?"

"No, One shilling."

"Two shilling?"

"Yes, that's fine, thank you," and the trade was done.

There was this road bridge that went out over the water to connect with the other side of the volcanic rim. Fishing off this bridge with my handline was the best fishing experience ever. I could see the fish as clearly as if they were in an aquarium and every so often, a moray eel would poke out and make a grab for the bait.

I played a little trick one day but I paid the price. One of the fishermen came ashore and in his catch were a couple of small sharks, not really big enough to sell when put beside some of the other fish. The fisherman must have noticed my eyes were like saucers when I saw them.

He laughed, picked them up by their tails in one hand and handed them to me.

"Buckshee, buckshee," he said. This was the local term for free.

When I took hold of them, he flicked his hand as if to say *"take them".* Indeed, I did, straight home and put them in the bath and left them! Well, the screams from my sisters brought everyone running. No one saw the funny side of the little adventure and I was told in no uncertain terms that they had to go. I was grounded for a whole week, unable to go down to the harbour.

From Crater, we moved to a more modern apartment in a slightly better area known as Ma-la. The overriding feature of Ma-la was the long, straight road that seemed to go on and on for ever, hence the name, The Ma-la Straight.

Our flat overlooked the road and beyond that, there was the Police Training Academy. We would spend hours on the balcony watching as the recruits were put through their paces. In the evenings, work gave way to volleyball for the Police cadets, and it wasn't long before my brother David was joining in with them. I would wander over with him but being too small to join in, I would take a ball and kick it against a wall.

View to the Police Training Academy next door

My father befriended one of the officers. He was a big and powerful chap. My sisters and I called him Charles Atlas, not his real name of course, but it suited him.

Charles would often visit and stay for drinks and meals and in return he would take us out to show us what Aden was like further afield.

I remember one such trip vividly. We were enroute to an oasis in the desert called Sheik Hoffman. We passed through a small village on the way. The centre of the village looked like the market-place and here there was a large crowd gathered with just about all of them chattering away excitedly.

Charles stopped the car and told us all to stay where we were. He got out of the car and walked over to the crowd; he was still wearing his uniform. The crowd parted, allowing him to get to the front and see the subject of the excitement.

Several minutes later, Charles reappeared, got into the car and we drove off. My father asked what the incident was.

"They had caught a thief," Charles said. *"Now he's facing a local on-the-spot trial, they will cut off his hand as punishment."*

"Goodness me," said my mother, *"Will he die?"*

"If he's lucky and someone takes care of his wound, he will be fine," said Charles. This was the way of things in third world countries at the beginning of the 1960s.

We didn't stay long at Ma-la. The much-awaited purpose-built accommodation for the refinery staff and their families was finished and we were on the list to move in. We had hit the jackpot!

Tarshine was a European/American settlement built right on the shores of the Red Sea. There was also a massive social complex complete with the biggest swimming pool I had ever seen with several diving areas and diving boards at three heights.

We were so close to the sea that one particular day when the authorities were depth-charging the bay with dynamite to clear out the sharks before re-laying the shark nets (a regular occurrence after the monsoons when sharks were often washed over the top of the nets), a massive lump of coral came crashing through the roof of our flat! Luckily no one was injured.

This place was paradise, I was now nine years old, but the idyllic lifestyle, complete with servants, had a price to pay. That price was the social interaction between the European and American residents of Aden. It was a non-stop round of parties, drink and more drink. The seeds were being sown right under our noses that would germinate, grow and destroy my family from within.

Tarshine was the holiday that never stopped. Our flat was the top of a block of four and from the balcony, we had a million-pound view looking out over the Indian Ocean, a view that was repeated from my bedroom.

A short walk of 20 yards would get us onto the beach; sun drenched golden sand filled the entire bay. The complex was a little further away, a two-minute stroll where we would find the swimming pools all but deserted and the main building blasting ice cool air conditioning.

As you looked out to sea, over to the right was a famous landmark, Elephant Rock. The end of the rocky outcrop was shaped like an elephant's trunk where the wave action of the sea had eroded a great gap between the trunk and rock face. I would spend hours and hours sitting and fishing at the base of the trunk, it was my idea of heaven.

My mother enjoyed an almost carefree lifestyle as well. Just after we moved into Tarshine, the locals were forever calling to see if there was any work. It wasn't long before we had our own cook, housemaid and laundry boy. Once it was clear that they were working at the house, no one else would call. They all lived locally and came every morning before we got out of bed.

We weren't alone in this. Every European household had their own local helpers, and our housekeeper helped me with my Arabic studies as she had a good command of English which made it easy for me to understand. When we had to leave, it was a very sad time saying goodbye; the cook in particular had become a very good friend of my mother's.

The beach was such an inviting place but it was impossible to walk on the sand in the afternoon without footwear. As the temperature of the sand would take the skin off your feet in seconds, flip flops were the order of the day.

The sea was constantly warm and inviting and an almost unbelievable deep blue colour but to go for a swim outside the shark nets would invariably invite disaster. Shark attacks, though not common, were an ever-present danger and more than one unlucky person paid the ultimate price while we were living there. The shark nets were a deterrent but as soon as the monsoon season hit, they would be taken in and all swimming banned. Before the nets were laid out again, the bay would be subjected to a barrage of depth charges to drive all the predators away before re-laying the protection.

One of my best friends lived just across the square from me. His name was Tone - short for Tony. Tone's father also worked for the government and was a colleague of my father. Together we explored every inch of the bay, caught every species of fish imaginable and had a new adventure every day. However, we always had to be on our guard for spiders, snakes and scorpions, the latter were everywhere. Some not as bad as the others but all were to be avoided. But try telling that to a couple of nine-year-olds.

On the whole we were very careful, but Tone came a cropper one day when we found a nest of scorpions. He was stung on the arm when he knelt down, not seeing the arachnid until it zapped him. We ran home as fast as we could - probably not the best thing to do in hindsight but we did. His mother took him straight to the medical centre where he spent the night.

It wasn't a serious sting, but it could have been much worse. The plus side of the incident is that it did teach us a very important lesson… scorpions were off list from that time onwards.

It wasn't long after that I took my own trip to the medical centre after a fishing trip ended badly – and I still have the significant scar on the underside of my right wrist to this day. After a couple of hours on my own at the elephant's trunk, enjoying some great fishing, I started back along the rocks to the beach. It was a reasonably long stretch over the jagged, barnacle covered terrain, about 100 yards or thereabouts. As I gingerly picked my way, my foot slipped and I went down, face first.

My instant reflex was to put my right arm out to lessen the impact with the rocks, my wrist landed on the razor-sharp barnacles, slicing the flesh open for four inches from the base of my hand going backwards up my arm. Of course it bled, and how it bled, my clothes and fishing towel were soaked in blood by the time I got back to the flat.

My father bundled me into the car and off we went to the medical centre. Ten stitches later and a lecture of *"Don't go fishing on your own again,"* we were on the way home with a sobering thought in my head. The doctor told me, in a very sombre way, that had I landed half an inch to the right on the barnacles, I would have severed the artery and not have been able to make it back to the beach before passing out from blood loss.

One evening in 1963, in our fourth year in Aden, my parents had gone to the European Club for a party, while I, along with my sisters and brother, went to the open-air cinema to watch a film. During the showing, the film was interrupted with a written message being flashed up on the screen asking for blood donors of a certain group to go immediately to the local hospital, as their blood was needed for an ongoing emergency. This was a common occurrence as the hospital was unable to keep stocks of blood very long.

The film resumed, people left the auditorium and we thought no more about it. When we arrived back home, a family friend was waiting to tell us that our father had suffered a massive internal bleed from a perforated ulcer and was undergoing surgery. The urgent blood request message had been for him.

It was touch and go, and twice my mother was told to prepare for the worst. But against the odds, my father pulled through and after two weeks in hospital, he was transferred to the RAF airbase at Khormaksar to be airlifted back to the UK as a medical emergency. CASEVAC, army speak for casualty evacuation.

My family and I followed several weeks later, this time by air, landing at Gatwick Airport. We were met by someone from the Civil Service, who took us to our new home. By this time, I was almost 11 years old.

Chapter Two

A Boy Loses his Mother

On his recovery, my father was appointed to the design team for the then new and revolutionary low flying bomber, the TSR2, based at RAF Boscombe Down in Wiltshire.

We settled in the beautiful Wiltshire town of Amesbury, a short drive from the cathedral city of Salisbury. My new school was in Amesbury.

Several weeks after my enrolment, it was the annual swimming gala. As a first-year student, schooling in the UK was a new concept for me. I had enjoyed almost daily, wild, open water swimming in the Indian Ocean for the past four years whilst in Aden. I was guessing not many of my peers at that time were as competent in the water.

I entered every class I could, even diving and holding my breath underwater. The results were unprecedented in the school's history... I came first in every class. This instantly launched me to superstar status among my peers and gained me respect from the teachers. I was loving life.

One of the adventure playgrounds for myself and a few mates was the magnificent Stonehenge, less than a couple of miles up the road from where we now lived. We played there most weekends. We had the freedom to come and go and do what we pleased. In those days, there was no governmental involvement, no visitor centre, no ropes fencing you off from the stones, there were no boundaries to playing and exploring.

Most of the time we had the place to ourselves. We took it for granted, not realising just how fortunate we were to be in such a privileged position. We were just a bunch of lads playing hide and seek amongst the stones of a 5,000-year-old ruin. I remember there was a large, low, flattish stone. We called this one the *slaughter stone* and it was pretty much the central point of all our games.

Apart from Stonehenge, there was loads to do in Amesbury, not least the fishing. The River Avon was a top river and anglers wishing to run a fly down the glides between the streamer weed would pay a hefty price tag for the pleasure. Me? No chance! Many is the time I would take myself off to the river with just my handline and a tub of worms.

The rewards were fat, plump trout, fresh as could be and a welcome treat for teatime. I knew these fish were the result of me poaching so my catch was always restricted to just one fish and it was always hidden under my jacket.

I remember one particular fish I caught was a monster and when I tied it up in the usual place under my jacket, the tail was hanging out below the bottom hem. I must have looked a sight for anyone spotting me walking home.

I was always aware that these were prime fishing waters, and I maintained my guard, easily hiding the tub of worms in a pocket and the handline inside my jacket if the need arose. I got away with this approach for many months until the day I was lost in my own thoughts watching a couple of trout moving sideways in and out of the streamer weed over the gravelly bottom. They emerged only to take a food morsel drifting in the current and then silently drifted back into the sanctuary of the weed.

I was so engrossed I didn't hear the country gent coming down the path behind me. There I stood, handline in hand complete with a wriggling worm attached, watching the river. It was then I was busted.

"What do you think you are doing young man?" said the gent, now joined by two black Labradors who came and sat either side of him.

Towering over me, the man was a formidable sight, straight out of a Victorian television drama. He stood about six foot tall, very slim and dressed in a tweed jacket with trousers that stopped just below his knees, where long socks took over, and a pair of boots on his feet. I remember he had a thick head of brown, well-cut, wavy hair. His eyes fixed on me through his heavy rimmed spectacles and he had the most remarkable moustache I had ever seen in my life.

He looked older than my father, much older. I just stood and stared, not offering any excuse for being there, my actions being obvious. The gent held out his right hand, gesticulating for me to give him the handline, which I did. He looked it over, shook his head and muttered to himself before looking at me and telling me to take the worm off and throw it in the water.

That done, the gent calmly and purposefully threw my handline into the river.

"Let that be a lesson to you, now clear off and if I ever catch you down here again, you'll be for it – understand?"

"Yes sir, sorry," I stuttered and off I ran, never to step foot on that stretch of the riverbank again.

There is a nice ending to this little escapade in my life. I never told my father what had happened, but then one day when we were both walking through Amesbury, I was horrified when the country gent appeared in front of us, coming in our direction. I tried to avoid his gaze and keep my eyes fixed on the pavement, but it wasn't to be.

"Now then young man, how have you been behaving, have you been down to my river since we met?" he suddenly asked. I met his stare, his eyes peering over the rim of his glasses as he towered over me looking down.

"No sir, not at all, I've learnt my lesson," I replied. It was the truth. My reply must have had the ring of truth in it as the gent pulled his hand out of his

pocket, reached for my hand a pressed a two-shilling piece into my palm. *"Well done lad, well done,"* he said and he was off… our paths never crossed again.

It was time to explain to my father and all he had to say was, *"I wondered why you hadn't been fishing lately."* It was shortly after this we moved out of Amesbury, but it was still close enough for me to go to the same school.

Our new house was at the top of a long driveway leading to a country mansion known as Snoddington Manor. I would spend a lot of time at the big house and I got on really well with the owner and his daughter. I would wander down most days to give her a hand with the chickens they had in one of the fields. She was a grown woman in her twenties but always had time to chat and show me the suits of armour and medieval weaponry that seemed to hang on every wall.

We lived in the *Lodge* in the manor grounds, a beautiful house with great gardens. I remember the borders all around the lawn, deep in foxgloves and lupins We were in the depths of the Wiltshire countryside with the village of Shipton Bellinger a good mile along the road… but this was halved if you cut through the fields.

Although the social life my parents enjoyed in Aden had now ended, my father was descending ever deeper into alcoholism. My parents were constantly arguing and as a result, my father would disappear to the *Boot,* a local pub in Shipton Bellinger, not to be seen again for many hours and usually returning in a drunk and abusive state. I hated these times.

He would fall asleep in the chair and if he was woken up, the perpetrator would have a high price to pay as he would direct all his hostility and anger in their direction. At times like this, my mother wouldn't be seen for days on end, preferring to stay out of the way in her bedroom. The girls, Kathleen, and Susan when she was home, would run the house, cleaning, shopping and cooking.

Amid a level of calm that presided over our household at Christmas 1964, my parents were planning a New Year's celebration with friends. My father left the house that evening at around 7pm for a trip to the *Boot*, promising to return to pick up our mother in time to go to the party.

Kathleen and I were waiting in with mum; she was ready and dressed for the party, my brother David was in service in the Royal Navy and Susan was busy at work in the hotel. As the evening wore on, I was feeling tired and took myself off to bed, kissing mum goodnight and wishing her a happy new year for when it arrived.

The new year didn't have the same feeling then as it does now. New Year's Day was just another working day… it wasn't until 1974 that it became an English bank holiday.

` clock in the hallway struck 2am but it wasn't
` the chimes that woke me, they were clear
background… in a murky sort of way.
she was pulling and pushing me,
get up, *"Peter, get up, mum's taken an
..ceed to go and get help."*

rlalf in, half out of sleep, the clock striking the hour and Kathleen shouting, I had no idea what was going on. Kathleen repeated herself, *"Mum's taken an overdose, you have to go and get help."* Kathleen ran back down the stairs; I quickly dressed and ran down the stairs myself to be confronted with my sister and mother fighting.

Mother was shouting to be left alone, Kathleen was trying to wrestle the bottles of pills from her. *"She's taken some pills Peter, get your bike and get help, PLEASE… GO!"*

At that moment, as I was running through the living room to get to the hallway and the outside door, my father appeared from upstairs, half dressed, shirt open to the waist and he was swaying, steadying his hand on the wall.

The signs were all there, he was drunk. *"Get back upstairs!"* he yelled at me. Now turning his attention to Kathleen, he grabbed her by the arm and marched her from the living room, up the stairs and told her to leave everything to him.

Not daring to confront our father when he had been drinking, we did as we were told. I went back into my bedroom and reflected on the last few minutes. There was silence from below as I lay back on my bed. I was drifting in and out of sleep for the rest for the night. It was still dark outside when I woke for the umpteenth time, but I was aware of someone outside my bedroom door talking.

I gently opened the door a little. It was Kathleen and she was speaking to a policeman. Pushing the door shut again, I turned and went to look out of my bedroom window. I saw a police car on the drive and a black van. I found out later that there was also an ambulance but that had gone.

I lay back on my bed, still fully clothed from earlier in the night when I heard noises from downstairs. The time escapes me. My head was an absolute mess. What happened last night? Was it real? Where's mum? All questions bouncing around with no way of confirming the answers.

I got off my bed, Kathleen was still there. Sitting on the top step, she had her back to me but turned when she heard me. Her eyes were red and bloodshot, she had been crying. *"Come into my room,"* she said, *"I need to tell you something."*

She gestured for me to get on her bed. *"Mum's dead,"* she said, very quietly, almost whispering, *"The overdose killed her, she died a short while ago."*

The Lodge: Peter's mother died in the ground floor front room

"Where is she?" I asked. By this time, it was sinking in that something catastrophic had taken place and I started crying. Kathleen was five years my senior. As we grew up together, we had a simple understanding that I would do as she said. She explained our mother had died even though police and ambulance men were trying to save her life. She had been taken away.

I could hear talking from below and my father sobbing. It was all hushed but from what I could make out, there were several strange voices. It was many years later that I was told the full horrific facts of that night, the night that changed my life forever.

It was Kathleen who told me the full story: She had been woken by the rhythmic sound of machinery coming from the living room. It was a stomach pump. Getting dressed, she went downstairs, but the policeman intercepted her and tried to comfort her. She saw other police officers, ambulance men and our father, sobbing.

He saw she was there and got up off the floor. *"I'm sorry, so sorry,"* he said. *"I fell asleep and woke up... it was too late, I'm sorry."*

The full horror hit Kathleen immediately. Our mother lay dying from an overdose of sleeping tablets while our father – who had shouted at us both to get back to bed, saying he would sort it – lay fast asleep in a drunken stupor on the floor as my mother's life slowly drifted away into eternal darkness... there was no help coming for her that night. My sister, Kathleen, kept this from me, only to tell me the complete story 55 years later.

The following days and weeks are, I'm afraid, a bit of a blur. We - my sisters, my father and I - went to my mother's cremation in Salisbury. Susan was working away from home and my sister Kathleen went back to Yorkshire to live with our grandmother. I stayed with our father.

During the preceding months, my maternal grandmother had grown to despise my father for the way he had treated her daughter - and now she blamed her suicide very much on his behaviour and drinking.

Peter's late mother pictured with the family dog Shandy

Within a month, we were away from the *Lodge* and headed back to Yorkshire. My father rented a flat within a large house along Shadwell Lane in Leeds. We were only there for a few months, but I doubt my father would remember as he was in a permanent state of drunkenness.

He woke up one evening in a foul mood well after 10pm and told me to go and get some butter from the shop. I tried to tell him it was late and that the shop would be closed but it did no good. I was sent out into the night, the wind was howling through the trees, it was pitch black.

I remember standing in the doorway until my eyes grew accustomed to the blackness before I set off. Away from the protection of the door, the rain was lashing down, stinging my face when I peered out of the security of my collar to get a clearer view. Shadwell Lane was a long, dark country road leading directly into the village of Shadwell.

There were no streetlights until you arrived in the village. I pulled my coat collar up as far as it would go and tried to hide my head from the elements. It was about a mile into Shadwell, and that night it took me about 25 minutes.

I had no need to hurry, I knew what I would find when I got there. My protestations to my father were well-founded - the shop was shut. I arrived back, soaked to the skin and empty-handed. My father had again slumped into a stupor, so I tiptoed past him, trying to be as quiet as I could and went to my bed.

During our time there - we arrived in early spring 1965 and stayed throughout the following summer - I joined a local cricket club as a junior player. I had been in love with the game of cricket for as long as I remember.

My brother David and I would play almost every day on the beach in Aden and now, living in Shadwell, I not only had the opportunity to play with lads my age, but also to go to Headingley to watch Yorkshire when I could scrape enough pennies together. Sometimes on the last day of a game, I was let in for nothing. Junior cricket in those days at Shadwell Cricket Club wasn't very competitive, with no proper games as such, it was just a series of practice sessions with a friendly game on Sunday mornings.

The sports day at the club was a great time for fun with every race you could imagine plus cricket games. It was all age-related so the older boys couldn't muscle in on us younger lads, giving us all a chance.

In the evening, there was a fancy-dress competition and I went as the Invisible Man. I borrowed my father's mackintosh overcoat and completely covered my head with a crepe bandage, wrapping it round and round from my neck to the top of my head, leaving two slits for my eyes so I could see where I was going. The outfit was completed with a borrowed trilby hat and pair of sunglasses. I thought I was the bee's knees as all the other lads had been dressed up by their parents, but my outfit was 100% my own effort. And I won! Five shillings – two half-crowns. Both nestled snugly in a small brown envelope in the palm of my hand.

I couldn't wait to get back home and tell my father. I was almost bursting as I ran the whole length of Shadwell Lane, I must have looked a proper sight, the Invisible Man running as fast as he could along a country lane. My father seemed impressed and genuinely pleased for me. He said he would keep my money safe for me if I wanted. *"Yes please,"* I replied naively. I never saw that little brown envelope again.

My new school was in the Leeds suburbs, Stainbeck, and I hated it. I was bullied nonstop, the name-calling, the odd foot thrust out as I was passing to trip me up. It was a shock and a real wake-up call as this type of behaviour was all previously unknown to me.

There was one lad, a good bit bigger than me. We had an instant mutual dislike of each other. He took every opportunity to take a dig, usually name calling. *"Snowflake"* was popular due to my fair, almost white hair. This would morph into *"Flaky."* This bigger lad got hold of me one day by my jacket collar and pushed me backwards until I was pressed up against the wall.

He wasn't alone, as there were five or six other boys with him, spurring him on to hit me. He looked down on me. He was about six inches taller and suddenly pushed his face forward until his forehead was touching the top of my head.

He told me in no uncertain ways that I wasn't welcome at the school. I'd only been there a week, a week too long. I tried to push him off but he dragged me down to the floor, kicked me once in the stomach and marched off with his band of thugs, laughing, leaving me on the corridor floor.

This was pure bullying for the sake of it. I had given this lad no excuse to treat me like this other than being enrolled into his class.

I soon started to skip school and found solace in the nearby Roundhay Park. The fishing there was excellent and I would spend day after day happily content with just myself for company. It was the old boathouse on Waterloo Lake. I would set up just where the rowing boats were moored and fish away to my heart's content.

Not having a keep net, I took a liberty with a waste bin, the sort that has a wire basket inside. I pulled out the basket, emptied the contents into another bin a short distance away and hey-presto, my own keep net. When I put it into the water just by my feet, the water level covered the bottom two feet of the basket, leaving about a foot above the surface. It was perfect.

There were times when I would simply take myself off to the lake without any fishing tackle; the quietness of the boating area early in the morning was enough for me to just sit and stare into the clear water as it shallowed towards the bank.

Small fish would go about their business unaware they were being watched so diligently. I would sit for hours staring into the water, trying very hard not to move or give my presence away for fear the fish would dart back to deeper water.

Dog walkers were a constant nuisance as the day wore on. This intrusion would cause the aquatic spectacle to be put on hold until the fish regained their confidence.

Living for the moment in this environment was my escape. The tranquillity of the scene soon had me thinking back to happier times with my mother, Aden and the fish under the road bridge in Crater and without realising, I would soon have a broad smile on my face.

Dad was still working at this point or at least he left the flat at a regular time each morning, so I was always left to my own devices when it came to getting up and off to school. I had my fishing rod hidden outside along with the bag of tackle.

My bait was bread and worms that I had dug from the gardens around the flat when dad was out. So, each day off I went, rod strapped to the crossbar of a bike I had borrowed from a cricketing friend in the village, and my tackle bag stuffed inside my school bag.

All was fine with the world until one teatime, there was a knock at the door and two men in suits were standing there.

I answered the door and was immediately asked to fetch my father. They introduced themselves as members of the education department and were here to see why I wasn't attending school.

My father invited them in to hear what they had to say. After an explanation from me revealing all about the peer group bullying, the two men listened and offered their sympathy and asked if I could leave the room while they spoke with my father. After a short while I was asked back in.

As they left, they apologised for the way I had been treated and promised that all would be resolved. I don't know whether or not they were true to their word - I never went back to the school and later that week we left the flat for the last time.

I was told to pack all my clothes, we loaded the car and set off. We didn't have many things in the flat, but the larger, bulkier things were left behind. I didn't realise it but we were doing a moonlight flit in daylight. We were to do it properly a week later.

Chapter Three
A Broken Family

With our time in Shadwell receding into history, my father and I started to live and sleep in the car. I can't remember the excuse my father gave me for doing so, I just remember the hunger and cold, and arriving each night in a different layby.

This was the time for a last walkabout, a stretch of the legs and a quick pee before trying to get some sleep. The nights were starting to get chilly; summer was behind us, and the days were beginning to draw in as we headed into September.

The first day was okay, just like any other day being out in the car. Dad pulled into the car park of a pub and told me to wait while he brought me something to eat. After ten minutes he appeared with a glass of pop and a packet of crisps. It was lunch time!

He went back into the pub and stayed for what seemed like ages, while I sat in the car and waited. I did get out at one point to ask to go to the toilet, taking my empty glass as an excuse. We would park in the most out of the way places and with only an old blanket to cover ourselves, we would wait for darkness, and sleep.

After a couple of nights on the road, we ended up in a car park in Shipley. The pub was called the *Black Bull*. I sat in the car while my father was drinking inside. He appeared with my lunch - a glass of pop and bag of crisps. This was becoming normal for us; many is the time the car would be my *safe zone* while dad was inside a pub drinking.

He came back to the car a couple of hours later and told me we would be staying here in the *Black Bull* for a few days. I can't remember the last time we had such good food, probably when Kathleen cooked it at home. I still thought about that part of my life as *home*.

For the last few months since my mum's death, we had eaten infrequently, mostly sandwiches, beans on toast, boiled eggs etc. Now we had good food and a comfy bed for the night. I'm not sure what my father told the landlord regarding the situation with a lone man and his 12-year-old son, but by that time I had little to say and never asked questions.

The *Black Bull* was a typical old-fashioned pub in the small town of Shipley, whose claim to fame was the world-renowned Salts Mill, a massive textile complex about a mile up the road. This mill and the surrounding cluster of houses and infrastructure were the creation of Sir Titus Salt. He created an entire village of houses complete with park, school, library, recreation area and a learning institute with outdoor sports facilities. He didn't stop there; he went on to name the surrounding streets after his children and family. In 1869 he was created a baronet by Queen Victoria, thus becoming Sir Titus Salt. This creation by the philanthropist was collectively known as the village of Saltaire, a joining of his name with the river Aire that flowed a short distance away, a stone's throw from Shipley town centre.

These few days in the *Black Bull* were just what the doctor ordered. The pub backed onto the Leeds-Liverpool canal and although we had little in the way of personal stuff in the car, I did have my fishing tackle. Again, it was bread and worms for bait and although the fishing was not as prolific as Roundhay Park, it was still my escape from reality.

My father would disappear through the day. I had no idea where he went but he always came back the worse for drink. We ate in the pub and then I would go to our room for the evening to sit and think or watch the black and white telly while my father stayed down in the bar drinking.

The room was sparse; two single beds with a small table separating them, two chairs and a table with the television on it. It was at the back of the pub with the window looking out onto the canal. I preferred looking out over the tow path into the dark murky depths of the water to try and spot the odd shoal of fish passing through. For me this was much better than watching the TV.

The bathroom was a communal one, a room away down the landing but as there were no other guests, we had it to ourselves. It was a simple room, one toilet, one wash basin and a bath. Getting in this bath was a pleasure. I had one every night of our stay.

I was shaken awake really early one morning after four or five days at the *Black Bull*. It was still pitch black outside. My father had his finger over his lips and was making a low, hardly detectable *"shush"* noise. He told me in a hushed whisper that we needed to get on the road early to start our journey as we were going to visit his brother, my Uncle Bob.

This was the first time I had heard dad speak about Uncle Bob since mum died.

I remember we made our way very quietly out of the room, dad carrying the suitcase as most of our stuff was already in the car. He didn't shut the bedroom door for fear of making a noise. Down into the bar area. It was pitch black with just a corner of the room lit up from the glow of the streetlight outside and I remember the rows of glasses on the bar, some half filled with stale beer and the stench of the same filling my nostrils.

As guests of the pub, dad had a key and the outside door at the side of the pub was only secured by a Yale type lock. Once outside, he left the door open but pushed back just enough so that it appeared to be closed. This time we had done a proper moonlight flit.

I had no idea how we were managing day-to-day living or getting fuel for the car. My father was not working now, and was often drunk, but we made our way to North Devon, living in the car on the way.

I will say this though. I knew my father was a very well-paid person whilst he was working and we, as a family, were never short of money. It could have been that he had access to his bank account when needed.

The M1 motorway was a recent development in England's transport infrastructure in the 1960s and was for the most part, our primary route south. The car was okay but with a top speed of just above walking pace, the journey had to be broken up into night stops.

By the time we crossed the county line into North Devon, we had been on the road for three days. The chance to get a wash and clean up never materialised. Food was from cafes and pub car parks, my pillow for the night was the back rest on my car seat.

The interior of the car was beginning to smell disgusting. Our personal hygiene was put on hold. In short, we stank, and our clothes were filthy dirty. I often wondered how my father had the nerve to go into shops and pubs. We were both a couple of homeless tramps. People would give us a second look as if their first glance couldn't be believed.

We eventually arrived in Berrynarbor, a small village about five miles east of Ilfracombe, and I met my uncle for the first time in many years. I had never met Uncle Bob's wife and had no idea he had two children, my cousins.

Our first meeting was frosty. Uncle Bob didn't seem very pleased to see us. I was taken inside the bungalow by my aunt. She introduced herself, *"Hello, I'm your Auntie Florry, come inside while your dad and uncle have a chat."*

The beautiful North Devon village of Berrynarbor

Uncle Bob stayed outside with my father and the pair of them had a very animated conversation in the garden. I could see them out of the window. My uncle was clearly making his point while my father did nothing but listen and nod his head.

Uncle Bob was a tubby, solid person, much shorter than my father and wore round spectacles with thick lenses that made his eyes look bigger than they were. He had a ruddy complexion with a bulbous nose and a wide grin that I came to know could be deceitful, as my time with the family continued through the coming months.

I once remember him telling me when I was just a youngster in short pants that when he was in the army, he played against the navy at rugby and like myself, loved to go fishing.

Uncle Bob and his family lived in a bungalow slightly outside the main thoroughfare of the village and on a steep hill. The garden wrapped itself around the bungalow with the right-hand side being extensive enough for both a vegetable garden and an area for the ducks - Uncle Bob kept Muscovy ducks and geese.

I never left my father's side over the coming days.

Then suddenly he dropped a bombshell that had a numbing effect on me and cast doubt on my future. He told me he was going away for a short while and would be leaving me with my uncle who would be looking after me as one of his family. I pleaded with dad to take me with him as my two cousins had already made it clear they did not want me to stay.

They had homed in on the atmosphere around my father and Uncle Bob. Both Uncle Bob and Auntie Florry didn't try to hide their feelings. We were a burden and, as my uncle and aunt seemed to resent my father, so their children assumed it was their role to also resent me.

Christine was the older child at 15 and Mary, a year younger. They were very close and often reminded me of the relationship I shared with Kathleen. Seeing them playing and talking together was reminiscent of our times together, times that had been suddenly and terminally cut short. The two siblings were very confident and sure of themselves and never tired of reminding me that it was their house.

Mary also had an axe to grind with me. It was her bedroom that I was sleeping in. She had to move in with Christine so that I could stay. Not the best of ways to meet my cousins.

My presence in Uncle Bob's home was uncomfortable. I knew that. The pain of losing my mother was still raw and that didn't help the situation. I would hide from social interaction with my cousins to become lost in my own thoughts. Tears and sometimes outbursts of uncontrollable crying were never far away once my father had gone.

I realised that this sort of behaviour on my part didn't help to build bridges and to some extent I was to blame for the fact that our relationship never really amounted to anything.

They must have thought I didn't want anything to do with them, but the truth was I just didn't know how to break into their world. I had nothing in common with them and so it became a case of them and me. I thought about my mother every single day. The memories were still very painful.

I had passed a milestone - the arrival into my years as a teenager, a right-of-passage into semi-adulthood, a time in my life that should have been witnessed by my mother but wasn't. My 13th birthday in April had come and gone but I couldn't care less. A few short months previously, I had a mother, a family and not a care in the world.

I often wondered how Kathleen was getting on. Not so much David and Susan, they were both on their own journey now and fending for themselves. I also didn't think about grandma. I knew as far as she was concerned, I wasn't her responsibility.

She had never shown anything like the level of attention and affection to me that she gave to Kathleen. There was no kindness from her quarter and the last few months had only proved to cement what she thought of me and my father.

Pretty quickly I was enrolled in a school in Ilfracombe, the same school my cousins went to, but they were a couple of years above me so thankfully our paths only crossed on the school bus. This school was nothing eventful for me… the recent past in my life was still very much to the fore in my thinking. The times with my father, so drunk he didn't know what he was doing or saying, had left me with very little to say. I had become one of life's watchers, content to sit and let things happen, offering no input or conversation. I had come to accept things without question.

I had begun to wet the bed, and in fear of ridicule, to my discredit, I tried to hide it. One morning Aunt Florry found the soiled bed sheets and brusquely let me know her thoughts on why my father had dumped me on them.

She was a hard woman, slightly taller than Uncle Bob, with wide hips that caused her to waddle from side to side as she walked. She was heavily built but not overly fat.

When she discovered the soiled sheets tucked away out of sight under the bed, she called me into the bedroom. I had a feeling this wasn't going to end well. She stood towering over me, hands on her hips, mouth drawn tight and eyes penetrating as she looked right through me.

"Come here you filthy little sod," she snapped.

I was on the verge of running away but my feet wouldn't move. I stood in the doorway now fully aware that my secret was out. Uncle Bob came up behind me asking what the matter was.

"Look at this," Florry said, *"No wonder his father didn't want him, the dirty little bugger has peed his bed and tried to cover it up."*

I was caught in the middle. I wanted my mum so badly at that moment. Uncle Bob slammed the flat of his hand round the back of my head, those thick, stubby fingers at the end of his massive hand sent me stumbling into the room, stopping just before I bumped into Aunt Florry. She lashed out herself, the flat of her hand catching me fairly and squarely across the left side of my face.

Not for the first time in recent months, I burst into uncontrollable crying and fell on the floor clutching the side of my face.

"You had better get a grip," spat aunt Florry, *"Pick up those sheets and take them to the kitchen,"* she ordered.

She then stepped over me and both she and Uncle Bob left me alone. The imprint of her hand was still visible on my face hours later as I prepared to get ready for bed.

This was the start of a horrendous period in my young life. The slightest mistake, a wrong word or error in judgement brought a swift and physical response from either my uncle or aunt, sometimes both.

I remember one day I was out with Uncle Bob. I had bruising and marks on my face from a previous disagreement as a result of my face meeting his hand. We met a couple out walking. I wasn't aware of their name or connection to my uncle and aunt.

They looked at me and asked what I had done to myself. Before I could reply, Uncle Bob took over, *"It was the dog,"* he said, almost laughing. *"Peter was running one way and the dog going the other, neither saw each other and bang! Poor Peter came off worse, he's mending well though."*

Uncle Bob put his arm around me in a fake display of concern and affection. I offered no explanation, I said nothing. I hated my life in Devon and I hated my uncle, he was an abuser, a bully, and now a liar.

With the break down in my relationship with my uncle and aunt since the discovery of the sheets, I was being singled out for blame on a regular basis, usually with punishment to follow.

My cousins followed suit and adapted a pack mentality with me as their prey and took every opportunity to make fun and ridicule me in front of their friends in the village. At first, I would be invited to go out and play with them and their friends, but it soon became clear I was only along as the entertainment. My cousins would take every opportunity to show me up and take the mickey. Their friends showed their allegiance by joining in.

I remember one distasteful joke they played on me not long after I had arrived. We were sitting in the church yard at Berrynarbor, a popular place to hang out. We were just talking about nothing in particular when a boy produced a plastic *Jif* lemon full of juice. Each of us in turn would have some squirted into our mouth while the others laughed at the facial expressions pulled by the drinker as the bitterness of the lemon juice reached their taste buds. I didn't know at the time but this was a set-up, a pre-arranged prank with me as the victim. There were two lemons. One for squirting real juice and one hidden in the lad's pocket. This one wasn't filled with lemon juice, but urine. When it was my turn to be squirted, the lad switched the lemons. The others knew what was going on. It was just me that was completely in the dark. They all thought it was hilarious, especially Christine and Mary who were laughing and pointing as I was coughing and retching, trying to clear my mouth. I never went out with them again after that, choosing my own company over them and their friends.

My time in Devon with my uncle was without doubt the low point of my life up until then. I was subjected to many violent beatings for no reason at all. If my uncle was in a bad mood, I would be the target.

There was one particular episode at the dinner table where I inadvertently disagreed with something that one of my cousins said. I was hit so hard between the shoulder blades with my uncle's open palm and I was sent clattering across the floor, chair and all. As I fell from the table, I reached out to steady myself, caught hold of the tablecloth and pulled the contents of the table onto the floor with me.

Aunt Florry exploded, she grabbed me by my arm with one hand and beat me about the head with the other while shouting at me. My cousins, both at the table, were laughing at my misfortune.

During my stay in Berrynarbor, I would take myself off on my own. I would either clean out the ducks to try and get into my uncle's good books or just set off walking for hours.

It wasn't far to the sea and I would spend my evenings and days just messing about on the rocks imagining that there were massive fish just under my feet and I had a fishing rod in my hands. Unfortunately, my fishing tackle was still in the back of dad's car!

It was on one of my walks I met a young lad and his sister. He was walking at the side of a pony with the lead in his hand while his sister rode it. Their names were Thomas and Sally. Tom was my age, 13, his sister Sally was 10. They lived on a farm just outside the village. I hadn't noticed them before as they had just returned home for a couple of weeks after a term at boarding school.

Even though Tom and I were the same age, I was slightly taller than him, but he made up for that by being a more solid build. Not puppy fat that so many young kids seem to have around their middles, but solid muscle.

Tom was a powerful lad, a legacy of his sports-oriented boarding school. He wore coveralls on just about every day we played out, standard protective clothing on the farm. He sported a mop of brown hair, which complemented his freckles. I don't think he ever bothered with a comb, his shock of unkempt hair summed him up perfectly; wild, adventurous and totally unmanageable.

Sally on the other hand was very different. Her hair was much lighter and trailed down her back, past her shoulders. She was the quiet one, but always had a smile. When she spoke, it was almost in an apologetic way, but when we were playing, she could shout and bellow as good as anyone.

Sally's pony, whose name escapes me, was the be-all and end-all of her existence, she loved that little horse so much. If she wasn't riding it, she was cleaning it; if she wasn't cleaning it, she was mucking out the stable; if she wasn't mucking out the stable, she was feeding it. The rest of the time she would play with me and Tom or come fishing with us. Just like her brother, Sally also wore coveralls day in and day out. It must have been a farmer's thing.

Getting to know Tom and Sally was the best thing that could have happened to me during those autumnal months. They didn't know my cousins, and I was thankful for that. We had some fantastic times before they went back to boarding school, days exploring the rocks and caves along the coast, walking with Sally while she rode her pony and the best times were fishing in their very own pond.

The farm had its own pond complete with a small island in the middle. It wasn't very big, about half the size of a cricket field, I thought, but there were fish in it and Tom had loads of fishing tackle, enough for the three of us. We had many competitions to see who could catch the most perch. There must have been some big perch in the pond, but I never saw them, only the results of their spawning. There were thousands and thousands of the stripey blighters, each about three to four inches long and they were ravenous for a little nip of a worm.

Getting away from my uncle's house for a few hours each day during the holidays kept my spirits up and gave me something to look forward to. I never told anyone where I would be going other than, *"I'm off to play in the rock pools."*

Tom and Sally's parents were also really nice people although I saw very little of their dad as he was always busy on the farm. I remember their kitchen in the farm house was massive. There was a great big table which looked lost in the middle of the floor, but it was warm and cosy, courtesy of one of the biggest cooking stoves I had ever seen in my life. Tom's mum used to make us proper, real lemonade and bake her own biscuits. She was a wonderful lady, very kind but also with an understanding manner.

I had never recounted my recent history to either Tom or Sally, but their mum seemed to know. Perhaps she was aware of the new lad who was living in the village with his uncle because his mother had passed away; I don't know, I never questioned it. The subject was still a very painful memory that I tried hard to block out.

My time with Tom and Sally was helping and I had begun to enjoy myself. But the holidays were over quickly and it was time for my two friends to return to their boarding school. They both went to the same one so sibling separation for them was never going to be an issue.

My visits to the farm didn't stop though. If there was enough daylight after school, I would take a walk down and brush the pony and maybe clean the stable if it hadn't already been done.

The weekends would invariably see me fishing in the pond. Tom's mum was used to seeing me around and I reached the stage where I was able to come and go as I pleased without question. I never took liberties. I only went inside the kitchen when invited. Other times, I would wander around the pond and sometimes just sit and watch the fish swimming around at the spot we used to have our fishing competitions.

On my way out of the farm, I'd wave if I saw anyone, visit the pony in the stables to say goodbye and as I passed the kitchen on my way home, I would tap on the window, smile, and I was off.

The Christmas holidays came around and coincided with one of the biggest snowfalls in many years. The festivities in my uncle's household were very one-sided. They carried on making plans as if I wasn't there. Aunt Florry would go into town Christmas shopping taking my cousins with her. I was never invited along. I remember on the run up to Christmas, Uncle Bob asked if I would like to go to work with him. He was a rep and called on businesses all around North Devon. Things are looking up I thought, *"Yes please, I would."*

Going with Uncle Bob was the lesser of two evils; staying with Aunt Florry was infinitely worse. My uncle drove a Ford Popular, a small car with an interesting window wiper mechanism; the slower the car went, the slower the wiper blades worked. I remember one day when we actually had a bit of fun in the car, and I enjoyed it.

We were going up Porlock Hill in the rain. The car began to slow down dramatically as it was a very steep hill. As the car slowed, the wipers followed suit by going really slowly. Uncle Bob said, *"If they get any slower Pete* (I liked it when he called me Pete, it was like I was beginning to be accepted) *you're going to have to sit on top and wipe the screen for me."* We both laughed.

Compared to modern cars, my uncle's was vintage with a capital V. I loved the way the trafficator came out of the side of the car between the front door and the back door to signal which direction the car was turning, and the satisfying clunk when it snapped back into the recess.

The working day for my uncle would involve going from town to town and visiting garages. He sold oil to the motor trade. I stayed in the car while he did his business, taking orders etc. We generally spoke little, and then it was nothing interesting. I once asked about my father. When was he coming to collect me? Uncle Bob closed that conversation down as quickly as it started. *"No idea, he'll come when he can,"* he said.

The week before Christmas I overheard Uncle Bob talking to Aunt Florry in the kitchen, *"I can't take him today, I have a meeting at our main office, I'll be hours."*

"I don't care," said Aunt Florry, *"Get him out from under my feet. I don't want him here, too much to do without running round after him."*

I knew they were talking about me. Uncle Bob lost the argument, and I spent the afternoon sat in a cold car in a car park, shivering. By the time Uncle Bob returned from his meeting, it was pitch black and the car was iced over. It took him 10 minutes to get it ready to drive. That was the last working day for him, as it was time to prepare for Christmas.

Christmas Day was a week before the first anniversary of my mother's suicide. I found myself constantly thinking about her, where we would be now if things had turned out differently. I remembered back to last Christmas at the *Lodge*. It was a good time, dad wasn't out every minute at the *Boot*, and a good atmosphere was all around.

The only downside was that David was away in the Navy. I remember going down to the big house with a Christmas card I had made and the daughter gave me a chocolate bar and some fruit.

This Christmas was a striking contrast… never before had I felt so much an outsider. I had no money, never had pocket money though my cousins did. I couldn't buy presents, but I did receive one, a scarf and glove set from Uncle Bob and Aunt Florry. I thanked them and asked if I could put them on and go out.

"You're welcome Pete, course you can," said Uncle Bob. I could detect a slight warmth in his voice and part of me wanted to stay but pulling my coat on I cheerfully bade them a short farewell. I didn't really want to go out in the cold, but it was an escape. My cousins both had a massive pile of presents waiting to be opened and I didn't want to be there when they did.

I was outside for a couple of hours, by which time it had started to snow a little, not massive flakes that children get so excited about, but more like light snow flurries. When I returned to the house, there was a light covering on the pavement and road. Apart from Christmas dinner, I spent the rest of the day in my room. My escape mechanism kicked in as I remembered the good times with mum, dad, Kathleen, David and Susan when we were in Aden.

We had terrific children's parties at the European Club. Santa used to arrive not on a reindeer, but on a camel. Each of us in turn were treated to a camel ride around the car park while all our friends and parents were clapping and singing in time to Christmas carols.

After Santa's camel was tethered and was being looked after by his elves, we would all go inside the club to receive our presents from the man in red himself. Then it was time for the games. Happy, happy times. When I came back to reality, my eyes were brimming with silent tears.

From Christmas until early January 1966, the roads for the most part were impassable, snow drifts had built up and walking was difficult. When the weather eventually eased off and I could get out with a bit of care, I set off for the farm. I hadn't seen Tom or Sally since a couple of days before Christmas and I was keen to see them before they went back to school.

It was a long walk that day trudging through the snow drifts was sapping my strength but on I went. Going down the drive, I could see the pond was frozen over and covered with snow. Tom's dad had obviously been out with his tractor and plough.

The drive was cleared and so was the courtyard leading to the house. I knocked on the kitchen door to be met by Tom's mum. She looked at me with a gentle smile and spoke softly. *"Oh Peter, I'm so sorry love, Tom and Sally went back this morning. Their dad drove them into Ilfracombe to get the train. Come in, you need a hot chocolate."* Of course, I was sad to hear I had missed my friends but the thought of a steaming mug of hot chocolate with mallows was a good consolation prize.

It was just Tom's mum and me sat in the kitchen that lunchtime. For no rhyme or reason, I found myself speaking about my own mum.

The anniversary of her death was just two days earlier. I spoke about the life we had in Aden and the past year leading up to me arriving in Berrynarbor. I was overcome with emotion as it was the first time I had spoken out loud about my mum. Tom's mother took hold of my hand across the table, *"Come here love, come here,"* she said.

She put her arms around me and gave me a cuddle, the first I had had since my own mother last cuddled me. It felt good, the warmth, the smell of her perfume, I didn't want her to let me go. For the first time in a long time someone was concerned for me, someone cared.

We talked a little more before I set off back to the village. I was sorry about not being able to see my friends.

"They'll soon be back," I told myself. Little did I know at that time, I would never see either of them again.

Chapter Four
Life Inside 539 GAR

A 1960s Wolsey 1500, almost identical to 539 GAR

I had no idea where my father was (I later discovered he was in prison) and I had no contact with either of my sisters, my grandmother or my brother, who was still serving in the Royal Navy.

In the space of a few short months, my family had disintegrated. I felt abandoned by my siblings and grandmother, a feeling that stayed with me for many years until I met and married Edwina and started my own family.

In early February 1966, my father suddenly appeared out of the blue. He stayed a couple of days before the two of us left Devon and headed back to Yorkshire, a trip that would take a lot longer than when we first came down.

He had acquired a new car, a Wolsey 1500. I remember the registration number to this day, 539 GAR. This little car was to be our home for the foreseeable future. We stayed overnight here and there and all the time, the atmosphere inside the car began to smell increasingly bad.

It wasn't pleasant by any means and reminded me of the old dustbins we had to drag to the roadside each week ready to be collected by the dustbin men. The days we lived in the car rolled into weeks and we seemed at one point to be going round in circles. It was as if my father was visiting the same area or people time after time.

During this period where the car was my home, the most I went out was a walk around the country lanes or around the streets in a small village. My father's health was deteriorating through alcoholism and by this time he was incontinent. The smell of stale urine was impregnating his clothes and the car seat. It was foul.

But leaving Devon was a life saver for me, I was quick to embrace life on the road and all that it brought with it, including the squalor. This new lifestyle was bearable only because it meant I was away from my uncle and his family. My only regret was knowing I would probably never be able to see Tom and Sally again.

I remember the car pulling into a pub car park on a beautiful but cool, sunny day. Dad disappeared inside, soon to reappear with his pint, a coke and packet of crisps for me. We sat at a table on the grass next to the car park. The adjacent table was occupied by two ladies enjoying the weather and a quiet drink. I sensed they were watching and talking about us, with a disapproving look on their faces. One of the two ladies held a handkerchief over her mouth and nose as they left their table and moved to the other side of the garden.

"I didn't like them anyway," I told my dad.

The sadness surrounding this incident was that it wasn't an isolated occurrence. The smell inside the car - the place we lived - was terrible. The stale stench of urine, unwashed bodies and piles of rubbish in the rear footwells all came together and seemed to cling to our clothing.

The car windows were open more times than not, but it didn't seem to do any good; as soon as they were wound up, the stench was back. My father and I had come to accept it and for most of the time, it was unnoticeable to us when we were actually in the car, but it was a situation that was very hard to escape from.

When we went into a shop or dad bought petrol, it was clear to see that we were the subject of attention.

People would see us and stare, the look on their faces said more than a hundred words ever could. I felt ashamed.

I had no idea where we were or where we were going. For the most part, I was just a passenger. Hunger came and went and I learned to be grateful for a bag of crisps or bar of chocolate for my dinner. I had settled into an existence where I didn't have a change of clothes for weeks or a proper wash either. The best I could manage would be a quick swill in the hand basin of a café or garage. I remember there was one café that ejected my father and me, telling us never to return. My father didn't complain. We left and drove on to the next village.

The nights were cold. We had one blanket each and only the clothes we had in our cases or on our backs. When we pulled up for the night, it was important to try and get to sleep as quickly as possible while the car was still warm inside, because it cooled very quickly. Dad would start the engine a couple of times through the night to warm us up but it soon got cold again.

I once asked why he couldn't leave it running all night. *"You want to wake up in the morning don't you?"* was his reply. To be honest, at that stage in my life, after what seemed like a lifetime on the road, I couldn't have cared less.

For some reason, we stayed fairly local to the roads and villages around North Devon. I was only aware of this because we visited a few public houses two or three times and my father met some so-called friends on several occasions though it still causes me concern when I try to understand how and where he met them in the first place.

This pattern of activity would all come to an end when we embarked on a longer than usual drive one morning.

After driving for most of the day, the car pulled up at a small shop. My father went inside and returned with some meat pies, something to drink and a few bags of crisps. It was beginning to get dark which meant it was time to find somewhere to stop for the night. We found a layby in one of the nearby country lanes and the bedding down ritual began.

A walk around the lane to stretch my legs, somewhere to have much-needed ablutions and then it was back to the car to get my head down in the hope I could get myself off to sleep before my father started snoring. The morning was never far away and my open eyes would greet dawn's first light through the streaming lines of condensation on the windows of the car before anyone or anything would wake me. My clothes and extra clothes were covering me right up to my neck but it was still perhaps the coldest time of the day.

Opening the door, I took myself off for a pee and some fresh air. This was a great time for me; the dawn chorus, the clear, fresh air filling my lungs giving me hope for a new day but the thought of crashing back to reality was always round the corner and would start as soon as I opened the door of the car and the stench hit.

Breakfast was never spoken about; it was rare that food of any description would be left over from the previous day, but I had managed to perfect the art of spotting lonely bottles of milk on people's doorsteps and - on the pretence of our need being greater - liberated them.

This wasn't the best way to start the day and our early starts certainly helped with our mini crime-wave, but the guilt never left me. I knew we were doing wrong. I took solace in the hope the owners of the milk would have understood our predicament had they been aware of it.

My father told me we were going to see a friend who he had telephoned the day before, adding that it was someone he knew. I didn't have a clue who he was talking about but as the day wore on, I could see as we passed various signposts that we were heading towards Salisbury. I guessed we would end up somewhere I was familiar with, and I was right.

The signpost showing *Shipton Bellinger* brought a flood of memories back. Most were memories I wanted to erase because the sight of all my familiar haunts, the roadside I walked along every single day going to and from the bus terminus for school, the entrance to the village and all the shops, each one of them had connections leading directly back to my mother.

On our way into the village, we drove past the road end to our old house, the *Lodge*. I could see it as clear as day up on top of the hill but on we drove. I turned to watch out of the back window until it disappeared from view.

We stopped in the car park of the *Boot*. My father went inside saying this is where he was meeting his friend and he would come out with something for me to eat. True to his word, he reappeared minutes later with a meat pie, a packet of crisps and a drink of pop. He told me he would be a long time as he had some business to take care of and if I wanted to go and find one of my friends, to be back for three o'clock.

It was almost 12 by the time I had polished off the pie and crisps. Time for a walk. I knew exactly where I was going, not to see any of my old friends. I didn't want them to see me as I was. I was going back to our house, the last place my family were all together.

Leaving the village, I hopped the wall and started up the field, the *Lodge* was visible in the distance but before I reached it, I had to scramble through the copse, a small but dense outcrop of trees and bushes. I knew the copse very well as I had often walked through it and played in it.

I continued following the sheep track through to the other side and then I started to climb the small slope in the field that would take me up to *Snoddington*

Manor. But before I reached it, my path would take a detour to the right which would bring me to the *Lodge*. I was walking parallel to the gravel drive between the *Lodge* and the manor, separated from the field by an iron fence.

As I got closer, I could hear voices. Walking quicker, I now had the fence on my immediate left. The *Lodge* was right there in front of me, exactly as I remembered it just over a year ago, a long time in my short life.

The voices belonged to two children who were playing on a swing on the lawn in front of the house. Their backs were to me and didn't know I was there. There was a cattle trough very close by. I sat down on a flat stone that was next to it with my back to the water trough and by looking over my left shoulder, I could see and hear what was going on.

The ground was cold as there had been a slight frost the previous night. I could see everything from my vantage point - the lawn where David and I used to play fight, the front window catch he would hang his sailor cap, and my bedroom window. I was lost in a sea of memories.

I wondered if the inside had changed much. If I stood up, I would be able to see inside the lounge window, the room where my mother had died the previous January. I sat in my own silence. It was a sad time, but there were no tears, not this time, just sadness and emptiness. My shoulders felt heavy.

There were no words I could say to myself, I just sat and stared, I had never felt so helpless.

The noise the children were making as they played seemed to get louder and it was clear they were enjoying themselves. It was at this point I wanted to leave them to enjoy the garden just as I used to. A final look.

The children seemed to be around six to eight years old and having a giggle at something. Then my eyes turned towards the house and my old bedroom window. I wondered if one of the children in front of me slept in it - an answer I would never get.

Retracing my steps down through the field, I stopped for a few minutes in the copse. There was the stump of the big old tree that I used to sit on. From this vantage point I could see everything – well, everything that mattered to me. I could look up and see the manor, over to the right, the *Lodge* and if I turned the other way, the road below taking cars into Shipton Bellinger and away to the right, the village itself. I could see the *Boot* in the distance and our car in the car park. It was time to go.

I later learned from my sister Kathleen that she also made a pilgrimage to the *Lodge,* but in her case, it was around 45 years later.

I was sat in the car when my father appeared from the doorway of the pub. He was drunk. His speech was slurred but at least he was walking in a straight line so I guessed he wasn't too drunk to drive.

Whenever he had been meeting his friends, not just this instance, he always came back drunk. It was my signal to withdraw into myself, to wrap myself in my invisible cocoon where I would turn in my seat, pull my clothes tight around me so that I could look out of the window as the countryside flashed by.

As we left Shipton Bellinger, I noticed for the first time that the grass verges on the roadside leading up to the *Lodge* were full of daffodils. I may have seen them earlier in the day but only now did I consciously recognise their presence. It was early April, and just a couple of days later it was my 14th birthday. It came and went without my father acknowledging it and I never mentioned it for fear of embarrassing him.

Eventually we headed north, back up the M1 motorway to Leeds. My father appeared to be on a mission as he seemed to drive with purpose to a specific housing estate on the outskirts of the city. After asking directions we ended up outside a house. I had no idea where we were or why we were there. I broke a self-imposed ruling and asked my father why we had stopped here but the answer was as I expected, very non-committal. He just told me to stay in the car and that he wouldn't be long.

He glanced back as he walked the 10 yards or so up the path to the door. A small middle-aged, balding man answered. His reaction was surprising after the way we had been received and treated since we left my uncle's place. The man took dad's hand and shook it for what seemed like ages, clearly pleased to see him. My father turned to me and beckoned me to come and join him. The middle-aged man was an old friend of dads.

To me it looked like this was the last throw of the dice for my dad. What would happen after this, I hated to think. I had never seen this man before nor heard my father talk of a friend in Leeds, but he seemed okay. His wife was a tall good-looking lady with neat, short black hair that really made her red lipstick stand out.

We were in the front room, a lovely blazing open fire roaring in the grate. I didn't want to leave. This was the warmest I had been since leaving Uncle Bob's place in Devon. The lady then asked if I would like a sandwich gesturing for me to follow her to the kitchen. *"Come on, let's have a cuppa while they talk,"* she said.

I left my father and his friend chatting like long lost pals eager to catch up. The lady offered me a dressing gown and asked if I would like a bath. *"Oh, yes please,"* I responded.

"Follow me," she said, *"Go into the bathroom and run yourself a bath then when you take your clothes off, pass them to me through the door and I'll put them in the wash for you. They'll be dry in a couple of hours."*

I thanked her profusely. Crikey I thought, a clean me and clean clothes to boot.

By the time I had finished in the bath and appeared in the dressing gown, it was clear dad had told his friend and his wife the sorry tale of our past few months, including my mother's death.

My father followed me into the bath and his clothes were also put in the wash, but I couldn't help overhearing a comment from the lady that they would be better off being burned. We were invited to stay for dinner and for the night. I was on the settee and dad was given an old camp bed to sleep on.

Our clothes were cleaned and ironed by the morning, and we were ready to go on our way.

"I wish there was more we could do," said dad's friend as he shook him by the hand, *"But you know how we are fixed. At least you have had a good meal inside you and clean clothes on your back, take care, the both of you."* As he said that he fixed me with a smile and a wink. The lady appeared from the kitchen with a bag. *"It isn't a lot,"* she said, *"Just sandwiches and biscuits to help you on your way."*

She put her arm round me and gave me the bag. *"You take care, promise,"* she said. I smiled and nodded. This act of kindness was a rare occurrence for me and my father. Thanking both of them in turn and shaking their hands, I turned away from the door and started down the garden path to the car. I was nice and clean and so were my clothes but the inside of the car was just as dirty as when we left it, and the smell, after not being in it since the day before, was overpoweringly awful. I left dad to say his goodbyes.

Industrial Keighley in the mid-1960s

He joined me minutes later and we set off again. From here it was just a matter of time before we ended up in Keighley.

That one night in Leeds was a godsend. I was in good spirits for the next day or so, buoyed up after a good and thorough wash, clean clothes and a good dinner inside me. Life was beginning to be bearable… but it wasn't going to last.

I did however ask my father to stop at the next layby we came to that had a rubbish bin. A clean up of the car was long overdue, we were clean and so it followed the car should be as well. I had no idea the amount of rubbish we had accumulated, bottles of pop, sweet and crisp packets, paper bags, the list was endless and embarrassing but at least it was all out of the car. Unfortunately, the smell was engrained in the upholstery and stayed with us.

We eventually found our way back to Keighley. I'm not certain about what happened next, I think my father had tried to make contact with my grandmother to see if I could stay with her. If that meeting ever took place, I was unaware of it. If it did, it must have been a negative outcome as I was never invited to stay.

Our time back in Keighley was restricted to going to a shop if we needed anything and then a few hours in the car park of a pub followed by a trip into the countryside so my father could sleep it off. Of course, in those days, there were no drink driving laws, so most of the time, my dad would drive when he was drunk.

I once remember him coming out of a pub in the early afternoon after being in there for around three hours when we were somewhere between Leeds and Keighley. He was in such a state that he couldn't walk steadily in a straight line.

I was terrified when he got in the car and started to fumble around with the key to start the engine, before driving away. The car was swaying all over the road, one car came towards us with the driver blasting his horn, causing us to swerve back onto our side of the road. I think dad himself was aware of his condition because it wasn't long before we stopped in a layby and he fell asleep with the car engine still running.

I reached across and turned the key back to stop it, got out of the car and went for a walk. I found a small pond, no one else was there so I just sat and watched the water.

Dad would be out of it for hours. I knew the stupor he got in and was an expert now on when he would come round. This time though I misjudged the time. I think the fresh air had had an effect. I had a little sleep and was woken by my father shouting for me. I made my way back to the car, where he was standing holding the driver's door open. He started to walk towards me and grabbed me by the arm.

"Get in," he barked, *"I need to be in town."* I couldn't remember the town, but the pub had an old vintage tractor in one corner of the car park. *"Go and play on the tractor, I won't be long,"* my father ordered.

I had barely reached the tractor when I heard a commotion at the pub doorway. A man had hold of my father by his jacket and was dragging him out into the car park where he hit him in the face and let him drop to the floor shouting something about begging and telling him to clear off.

I ran to my father as he was getting to his feet

"That was nothing, don't worry about it," he said as we made our way back to the car and away. He never

told me what the argument was about and I never asked. I did have a guess though that he was out of cash at that point and tried to get a drink by unconventional means. It wasn't only drink that sometimes came by unconventional means. I know of at least two instances when he filled the car up with petrol and made a quick exit before paying!

Now, back in Keighley, our daily routine was unfolding but as this was my hometown, I asked if we could go and look at our old house where we used to live before moving to York and then on to Aden.

We drove out of Keighley, up the steep hill until we were in Long Lee. We sat outside the house for a short while, under the shadow of the big electricity pylon at Royd House Walk. We both sat, just looking. The memories came flooding back.

My father must have been having a hard time coming to terms with where we were. He started crying, and in no time at all he was inconsolable. His forehead rested on the back of his hands as he gripped the steering wheel tighter and tighter. It must have been around fifteen minutes before he stopped sobbing and calmed down. He looked at me, his eyes bloodshot and snot running down his face into his mouth. He wiped it away with his jacket sleeve. I thought he was going to say something, but the moment was lost when he said he had to meet someone in the *Globe*.

The *Globe* was a popular pub on the corner of Parkwood Street, one of my father's old haunts. When we got there, he told me to go for a walk into town and he would meet me at the bottom of West Lane next to the Working Men's Club. After a wander about the town, I went over to West Lane where dad's car was already parked, so I guessed where he was and climbed into the car.

Grandma lived halfway up West Lane, a long, steep hill. I reckoned I could be there in 10 minutes, and would be able to see Kathleen, I told myself. Instead of going, I sat there thinking about it. When dad appeared, I asked if we could go and see Kathleen but no joy.

We ended up at Oakworth, a few of miles out of Keighley where we parked up for the night. It was alright for my drunken father. As soon as he shut his eyes, he was snoring like an animal, but it took me a long time to drop off, not just now but every night.

There was no way I could have known it but that night, parked up at the side of the crematorium in Oakworth, was to be my last night on the road.

I usually woke up first and got out of the car if it wasn't raining, as the fresh air was good. I would wander around stretching my legs while looking for a place to have a pee before going back.

The time we had spent on the road since leaving Devon had been hard on both of us but with no alternative and my father becoming more and more incapable, there wasn't a quick fix. No remedy, no one knew where I was and I had no idea how to get in touch with my brother and sisters without physically turning up on grandmother's doorstep. That was never going to be an option.

Apart from the makeover both my father and I had in Leeds, which turned out to be an oasis in our wilderness, our journey was not at all enjoyable. The smell of stale body fluids, going without food and, worst of all, the cold at night.

Drifting off to sleep was a merciful occurrence but short-lived as I would be wrenched back to consciousness, shivering and not able or wanting to move in case a cold blast of air crept into and under my clothes. Hunger was an ever-present state and I'd lost a lot of weight. I wasn't podgy at the best of times but now, just skin and bone.

Dad started the car to go into town. We were going down Oakworth Road, heading for Keighley when a white car with a red flash down each side, a Triumph Herald, overtook us and pulled sharply in front to stop us. I remember my father shouting and swearing at the other driver as he slammed on his brakes and swerved up onto the pavement, stopping before we hit the stone wall at the side of the road.

The driver of the car got out, a big man, too big, I remember thinking, for that little car. He wore a short, black coat and a black hat on his head, eyes framed by dark rimmed glasses.

My father got out, shouting at the other driver but very soon calmed down and they both talked for several minutes, leaving me wondering what was going on. Mr Black Hat was gesticulating a lot and kept pointing with the flat of his hand over in my direction. I knew they were talking about me.

The man eventually came to my side and knelt down, gesturing with his hand for me to wind the window down. I noticed he momentarily recoiled as the full, pungent odour of the car's atmosphere hit him.

Regaining his composure, he was smiling as he asked me to get out of the car. He was a nice guy with a really soft, kind voice and I liked him from the off. He told me his name was Mr Watson and he knew of a place in Ilkley, a home for children that would soon be going on holiday to Cleethorpes. Would I like to go with them?

My father at this point had tears rolling down his face. His eyes were bloodshot. I noticed he was blinking a lot. I looked quizzically at him, but he gestured at me to go with the man.

He didn't speak. I was beginning to feel like the little silver ball in a pin ball machine, bouncing from one situation to another. I was on my way into the care system. It was Saturday 28th May. It had been 13 weeks since we had left my uncle's place in Devon.

Chapter Five

Into the Care System

It was as we were driving to the children's home and in answer to some of my questions, I was told that the Social Services had received a call from a relative to say I was living in a car... I took that relative to be my grandmother.

The children's home, *Hill Top* in Ilkley, was at the very top of the steep and long Wells Road leading out of the town towards the famous moors. Where the road met the moors, it deflected to the right over a cattle grid leading onto Westwood Drive.

Hill Top was a large, imposing building with four floors. The great and ornate iron gates were open, and we drove in, following the drive round to the left and then to the right pulling up outside the front door on the other side of the home.

I thought I was just coming here for a holiday and then would be taken back to my dad. How wrong I was.

My first thoughts and all my thoughts were regarding the holiday I was promised. It never entered my head that this was to be my home until I left school a few years later.

As I got out of Mr Watson's car, I could feel the eyes of all the other boys on me, some were outside and some staring through the windows. I didn't return their gaze, there was a gnawing inside me… I felt like fresh meat.

I was introduced to the children's home superintendent, from now on referred to simply as the *Super*. His name was Colin West, and his wife Doreen was the matron.

Hill Top children's home in Ilkley

There were also two support workers that lived in, Mary Green and Susan Copeland, both referred to just as *Miss*. Additionally there were kitchen staff and cleaners that lived locally.

The atmosphere was noticeably strange. None of the other boys seemed to be overly vocal. I could see them passing us with inquisitive glances and then scurrying off in silence.

The *Super* was a short, very round man with heavy spectacles that were forever finding a way to slide down the bridge of his nose. I don't know why he had them as most of the time he was peering over the top of them. He seemed to be continuously sweating and he could do with losing a bit of weight, I thought to myself. He was always mopping his brow with a handkerchief. I noticed that his eyes would get very wide as he talked. In the instant I met him, I disliked him.

I guess he was aged 50 plus and *Matron* looked to me to be in her middle to late 50s, I had no way of knowing as it was just my impression. She had oversized front upper teeth that would always be visible when she rested her mouth. Like the *Super*, she too wore glasses, fancy specs that seemed to blend in with her face and hair. Their office was just inside the front door. As Mr Watson and I first arrived I remember a boy was standing outside the office looking out of place and unsure what to. Upon seeing us, the *Super* told him quickly to go.

For the first few days, I had a mixed collection of thoughts going round in my head. Pleased at last I had a regular bed to sleep in, pleased at last I was getting regular meals, pleased at last that I was wearing clean clothes all the time and pleased at last that I was among like-minded souls who were in the same crazy, mixed-up part of their lives.

But these positive thoughts were tempered with thoughts of my family, or Kathleen mostly, who I knew was just 11 miles away. I knew beyond doubt that there was a spare bedroom in my grandmother's house. There was a direct bus service from Keighley to Ilkley… but no one came.

It was clear from the outset that my grandmother wanted nothing to do with me or my father; my guilt in this matter was simply from association. This was something that was to haunt me throughout the following years until I eventually left the care system.

In the first few weeks, I cried myself to sleep every night. It wasn't a heavy, sobbing cry but my eyes would be watering, and my nose would start to run. But I held it in, and no one would know what I was doing, because by now I knew it was a sign of weakness and I was conscious that I shared my room with three others.

I did have one visit shortly after I moved into *Hill Top*. My grandmother brought Kathleen to visit me. My heart flew, I hadn't realised how much I had missed her. I was so happy I even thought that grandma was beginning to like me, and that these visits might become regular. Had I known that was to be my first and only visit from my family, I wouldn't have wanted to carry on living. In my mixed-up way of thinking, I wanted to be with my mum, and would have found a way out – I'm certain.

It was many years later I learned that my grandmother had told my sister that my father had been to collect me from the children's home, and that no one knew where I was. I didn't know this at the time, but from that moment on, I was completely on my own. By this time, I had just turned 14 years old.

After a few days in my new home, Mr Watson paid me a visit to see how I was getting on. He took me that day to Wakefield to a massive warehouse where I was kitted out with clothes. Not new clothes, but old, used ones that in some cases had been damaged and repaired but all were clean, although most had name tags of the previous owner that had to be removed and replaced with my own.

Life at the home was a mixture of hand-me-downs in the clothes and shoes stakes.

When I went to Wakefield, it took the best part of the day and during the journey back to Ilkley, I found out that my intended stay was going to be longer than anticipated. I had several shirts, two pairs of shoes and three pairs of trousers. I asked Mr Watson why I had so much stuff when my father could come and get me anytime.

He looked at me and said, *"Just a precaution Peter. We don't know where your father is at the moment so we will be looking after you.*

"Your dad will have to be able to show us that he can look after and support you again before you can go and live with him.

"You like it at the home, don't you?" he added.

Once I was settled in care, any new clothes I needed were supplied in-house. There was a store cupboard on the top floor where the staff had their rooms. Here all serviceable clothing and shoes that were no longer required were cleaned and put away ready for their next owner. Nothing went to waste.

I settled into my new life with an open mind. I still found it difficult to express myself but drew comfort that several of my inmates had also suffered the loss of a family member. I wasn't alone in that respect.

Not long after my arrival at the home, I started school at Ilkley Secondary Modern on Valley Drive.

I wore a silver ring that belonged to my mother and it proved to be the most difficult thing to get off. I was still growing and my fingers had become slightly thicker due to me eating regular meals and it was beginning to show. The *Super* was aware of the ring and on more than one occasion intimated he would cut it off my finger.

One teatime, we were all sat at our tables in the dining room. There were four separate tables, each capable of seating six boys, and one for the staff.

On entering the dining room, you were faced with two tables on the far wall, separated by a door that led into the cloakroom and eventually outside. To the right of the door was a small table with all the plates and cutlery, which in turn was next to the dumb waiter that brought the food up from the kitchen below.

To the left of the door was the fourth table for us children and at the top, underneath the windows was the longest table which the *Super*, *Matron*, and the two live-in staff would be seated at. From their vantage point, they could watch and keep an eye on every child at mealtimes.

The *Super* shouted to me, *"Foster,* (it was always surnames, no first names, no terms of endearment at all) *what did they say to you about your ring at school?"*. I was surprised at this level of interest and replied that it belonged to my mother, and I had been told that *"under the circumstances"* I could keep it on.

What followed was my first public ridiculing from the *Super* (there were to be countless other episodes). *"Wuhoooo,"* he laughed, *"Under the circumstances"*. He mimicked me in a high-pitched schoolboy voice. *"Where did you learn to talk like that?"* He went on to poke fun at me until the other boys stopped laughing.

He was a hateful figure, as round as he was tall, and he seemed to revel in dishing out orders and punishment. The saving grace was that each of us were treated the same by the *Super* and to a lesser extent, his wife, the *Matron*. And the support staff were also at times unbearable. They most certainly had their favourites. If you weren't on the list, life was difficult in the form of extra duties, ridicule and put downs.

The senior member of staff was a lady called Mary Green or MG for short. It was only the *Super*, *Matron* and the other staff who were allowed to use MG as a recognised referral. For us, the lads, it was always Miss Green or simply Miss.

MG stood about five foot nine inches tall with a slim build and shoulder length dark, straight hair, almost black. She was head and shoulders above the other staff but even MG would not be seen to disagree or act differently from the way things were run at the home.

But in hindsight I'm as sure as I can be that if MG had been in sole charge, the experience of life at *Hill Top* might have been different.

Many is the time when the *Super* was having a go at one of the lads, I would catch sight of MG wincing in disapproval, but she remained a loyal member of staff, respecting the hierarchy. In line with the rest of the regime, MG was hard but fair. If you were misbehaving, she could reduce you to a whimpering mess with her withering stare and savage tongue. But if you were the victim, the attention was much more muted, almost to the point of being caring... but acts of compassion in the home were non-existent and her behaviour would always stop just short of any form of compassionate display.

Many is the time I witnessed a situation involving MG and one of the younger lads. She would show a tenderness if the lad was upset and talk gently but in reality, all the lad needed was a hug. I knew very little of the home life that the live-in staff had although I was always under the impression that neither were married and neither had any children of their own which may explain the lack of empathy towards the boys, particularly the younger ones.

Miss Copeland on the other hand was cut from different cloth. She was slightly shorter with lighter hair that went down her back past her shoulders. She had a most distinguishing feature; her nostrils naturally flared, reminding me of *Pug* from the *Beano's Bash St Kids*. No one ever pointed this out to her. No one would dare.

Miss Copeland had her favourite lads. For the rest of us, we treated her with this in mind, trying very hard not to incur her wrath. The slightest infringement would see her sending us to stand outside the *Super's* office door for some punishment or other to be handed down after she re-told an embellished account of the misdemeanour.

Her own troop were rewarded with the biggest portions of pudding, the easier jobs and never failing a rota inspection.

I once happened upon both MG and Miss Copeland talking together. They were unaware I was close by and although I couldn't get the full gist of the conversation, it was clear that MG was tearing a strip off Miss Copeland after seeing her with some of the boys and then treating others in a different way.

The live-in staff would work a week or so and then have two days off at home. When MG was away, Miss Copeland was truly difficult, so the best course of action for us lads was to stay well out of her way.

There was a time when a third live-in member of staff came. There had been an influx of boys into the home so an extra pair of hands was needed. Her surname escapes me, but I do remember her first name was Christine. She was a nice, seemingly caring person, who made an effort to get to know the boys.

From our perspective, this was a most welcome change. So much so that often she could be found doing her duties with a gaggle of the home's young lads in attendance. She was beginning to take on the role, even though unintentionally, of a surrogate mother.

Many is the time she would get a group of lads together when it was quiet and gather them in the television room and read them a story. This interaction between the staff and us lads was like a breath of fresh air but it didn't last long. The other two staff took a dislike to the familiarity and would take every opportunity to disrupt such gatherings. With Miss Copeland taking the lead, it wasn't long before her bullying and downright unkindness caused

Christine to leave. She had lasted just three months, and we were back to just two live-in staff and it stayed like that for the rest of the time I was there.

One Saturday, an old boy turned up out of the blue for a random visit. Strangely the *Super* and *Matron* spent a lot of time with him throughout the morning, seemingly not wanting him to be on his own. I really didn't know if they were pleased to see him and liked his company but with the value of hindsight, it was clear they were unable to trust him.

He was a big lad, now in his 20s with black, greased hair, leather studded jacket and jeans with black ankle boots completing his rigout. But the aura he projected as he strutted round the home totally evaporated as when he spoke, he had a pronounced, squeaky stammer. On the exterior, he looked every inch a hard-nosed rocker but in reality, he was just a wannabe.

Paul was his name and he was invited to stay for lunch. During the afternoon after kitchen duties, we (the lads) had some free time up on the lawn for a kick about. Paul had shaken the *Super* and *Matron* off and came to join us, but not the senior lads.

He seemed to have attracted the attention of the younger ones who followed him everywhere, listening to his exaggerated stories of when he was living in the home himself and what he used to get up to. He knew the layout of the grounds and the out-of-bounds areas as well. With wild stories of campfires and hiding from the staff, Paul and a small group of three youngsters disappeared under the wire fence and into the bushes beyond. Out of sight and into the out-of-bounds area.

We just let them get on with it. We were having a good game and to be honest, our attention didn't stretch to the antics of the younger boys or indeed Paul, who we had grown tired of with all his bragging and fanciful stories. After a while, two of the three younger boys, Michael and his brother Stephen, appeared from the out-of-bounds area. Both were shouting for my pal, Stewart.

They told him they had built a den in the bushes and Paul had sent them off to look for more branches but when they returned the entrance to the den had been blocked off. They pulled a branch away and saw Paul sexually abusing the other lad.

Both were minus trousers. By this time, I had joined Stewart, and we both told the brothers to run and fetch the *Super*, while we would find out what was happening.

We shot under the wire fence, shouting for the lad still in the den. He shouted back and we found him in double quick time, time enough to see Paul zipping up his jeans. Paul was indeed a big, solid lad and neither Stewart nor myself were entertaining the thought of confronting him as our immediate concern was for the young lad he was sexually molesting.

We quickly put ourselves between him and Paul and marched him safely back to the lawn. The *Super* was just arriving. He took the lads to one side, asked them what was going on and then sent them inside to see *Matron*. Paul appeared, he had to, there was no other way out or off the premises. The *Super* simply ordered Paul, *"My office. Now."* They both disappeared off the lawn and into the home. We never saw Paul again after that.

The incident was never mentioned. The young lads involved in the whole sordid affair were never interviewed by the police. In fact, I don't think the matter was ever reported. It was as if it had never happened.

I remember a new face appeared in our ranks one afternoon, a lad no more than 10 years old. His face was all blotchy and his eyes were puffed up. I recognised the familiar symptoms and I really felt sorry for the youngster. His mother, a single parent, had been rushed into hospital leaving Social Services to take care of her son.

He was taken into care and brought to *Hill Top* for as long as his mother was in hospital and unable to care for him. Completely and utterly alone with everyone around him complete strangers, the lad was worried to death about his mother, too frightened to speak and was constantly crying.

He sat on my table for his first meal. If I remember rightly, we were having some sort of macaroni cheese. The young lad said he didn't like cheese and couldn't eat it.

"Fine," said the *Super*, *"But there's no pudding until you do."* The young lad still couldn't eat it and after tea, left the table when we all did but not before he was given a lecture from the *Super* about how he should be thankful he was getting fed.

The poor lad was in floods of tears, and he just wanted his mother. I knew how that felt. He did get some biscuits and a drink of milk before going to bed. In the morning, we were seated at our breakfast table and any thoughts that the young lad had of today being a bit better than yesterday were cruelly ripped away when the *Super* came and placed a plate of food in front of the boy. It was last night's macaroni cheese and still on the same plate. It was the same meal he had refused at yesterday's teatime, only this time, it was clap cold.

Again, he couldn't eat the cheese, and left the table without having any breakfast and he wasn't offered any substitute. His next meal was lunch, thankfully the cheese had been thrown out after breakfast by one of the kitchen ladies who hadn't realised it was needed. The young lad went from lunch on the day he arrived to lunch the following day with just a couple of biscuits and a glass of milk to sustain him.

This type of occurrence arose every day, and in hindsight, I'm disappointed with myself that I didn't stand up for some of those youngsters at the time but to do so would have brought swift retribution.

Another occasion when I was the victim of the *Super's* cruel attention was when I was studying for my exams in the 5th form at school. My geography topic was Australia. I spent every waking hour through the holidays doing research both from *Hill Top* and visiting the library in Ilkley when allowed. I had a small table in the corner of the dining room where I did my schoolwork, because it was usually the quietest room. It was out of bounds unless you were walking through to get to the cloak room, so for the most part, ticked the right boxes of peace and quiet for me.

But this day, there was a visitor to the home, who he was or what he was doing was of no interest to me, I didn't even know his name.

I was at my table as usual; the other children would have been down in Ilkley or out playing football. Then out of the blue, the visitor appeared in the dining room. I never knew his name so for the sake of this book I'll call him Mr Jones.

Mr Jones came into the dining room and walked over towards my table and started asking questions about what I was doing. I was deep in thought and lost in my project and really didn't want to be distracted so I simply and politely told him I was trying to complete my exam project for school.

Mr Jones reached over without invitation and picked up some of my research notes off the desk at the same time as the *Super* came into the room. Not saying anything to me, the *Super* began talking to Mr Jones who in turn said that this was excellent work from the young man. That was it, nothing else. The two of them left me in peace and went about their other business.

At tea that evening, when we were all sat down waiting for our food and Mr Jones was long gone, the *Super* started to mock me. Speaking to all but no one in particular, and in a pronounced, raised voice, he said, *"We had a visitor today, you should have seen Foster showing off,"* (in his idiotic and hateful mimicking voice).

"Oh, sir, do you want to see what I'm doing? It's a project for school, look at it, it's taken me ages." My hatred for that man was growing by the day.

Several of the younger children had a bed-wetting problem, a condition that had afflicted myself briefly just after my mother died. I had no control once I had gone to bed and fallen asleep and I knew full well that the younger children also had no control, but they still paid a high price for wetting the bed. The *Super* would tell the unfortunate child to go to the bathroom where a bath had been run with cold water.

The child was made to get into the bath and wash himself under the watchful gaze of the *Super* as he sat on his chair located in the corner of the bathroom.

He would turn the chair round so it was facing the wall and sit on it, legs straddled across the seat, with his back facing the wall and his arms spread on top of the backrest of the chair. From this position, the *Super* could see down the full length of the wash basins - six in total - and a large bath at the end. On the other side of the room were a couple of shower cubicles. All came under his gaze.

There was no privacy in the bathroom, personal washing and cleaning times were scheduled in groups, each group was supervised by the *Super*.

This is all a snapshot of what life in *Hill Top* children's home was like for me and many other boys. And from what I have read as an adult it was replicated for hundreds more children at many other such homes right across mainland Great Britain.

Chapter Six

Miss Mary Weatherall

Ilkley Secondary Modern School

I lkley Secondary Modern, Valley Drive, was my place of contentment, my escape if you like. My class teacher was a giant among her peers, Miss Mary Weatherall.

Miss Weatherall was a special person who could bring out the best in her pupils. She was also a compassionate and caring lady who made my life in care so much more bearable. I am indebted to her to this very day.

Being in care severely restricted any social interaction with friends and people who might become friends. Miss Weatherall recognised the failings of the system and for over two years, she became not only my teacher but my friend.

If I close my eyes, I can picture her now. She wasn't a tall lady - I would say about five feet four or thereabouts. Her hair was always immaculately presented, and her glasses complemented her complexion. I remember she had high cheekbones that always gave the impression she was smiling, but no one would think that was a sign that she was a soft touch. Far from it, Miss Weatherall could be a very hard taskmaster at times.

She was my form mistress for two years, in the fourth and fifth year. My classmates and I were the envy of the school, as everyone wanted *Ma Weatherall* as she was affectionally known, as their teacher.

English was my topic and also that of Miss Weatherall so we had an understanding, a common thread, if you like. I would always pull out the stops to complete my work and present it in good order, something I'm sure that was appreciated. Although she appeared to take an interest in me, it was never evident to the rest of the class. Indeed, sometimes it was as if I was singled out for scrutiny more times than the others.

I recently met some of my old classmates for a 50-year reunion and they were unaware of the extracurricular relationship that Miss Weatherall and I shared out of school.

I wasn't aware that she had made an approach to the authorities to request that I could visit her for tea on a weekend in her home. She had never spoken to me about it until I was told by the *Super* that I had an invitation to tea from my schoolteacher. The next day at school, I made my way to the classroom early, well before the bell and before everybody arrived so that I could thank her with no one else present.

That was the start of several visits. They weren't every week, but very pleasantly remained an exciting time to look forward to. I loved her teas. Cream cakes and strawberries were in very short supply at the children's home.

I valued these times. There was no pressure, no sharing, this was my time and rightly or wrongly, I thought, my place. I felt secure in Miss Weatherall's company but with everything good that occurred in the children's home, there was a price to pay and for several days after such a visit, I wasn't *Foster* to the *Super*, I was "*teacher's pet.*"

Miss Weatherall and I enjoyed several awayday trips together during the summer, mostly ending up in the museum or some other culturally informative place.

It wasn't a case of just turn up and off we went. As you would expect there was a fair amount of red tape to be completed but once there was a precedent in place, it became easier and less troublesome.

My favourite trip involved us going to York. The Viking centre and the Minster were must-see places and we also went boating. It seemed the most natural thing in the world, me rowing along with Miss Weatherall sitting in the stern enjoying the summer sunshine and bird song.

I remember going under a massive bank of willow trees that were growing out over the water and for a moment the entire sun was blocked out and it was decidedly cooler, but we sailed on and found the sunshine again. I didn't feel privileged at this attention from my teacher, but I did value the time we spent together. At each parting, as I left to go back to the home, she pressed a book into my hand to read.

I grew fond of Miss Weatherall in a respectful way and I never took liberties. I always addressed her as *"Miss"* and I used her full name in school. I think the fact that I didn't take advantage of the situation was met with approval from her.

I often wonder what may have happened if I had told her about life at the children's home, but I never did. What happened there, stayed there. The consequences of *talking out of school* were too frightening to bear.

Life in care was emotionally cold, each child was just a surname. In one respect, I was fortunate in that

I became the oldest inmate 18 months before I left. This position didn't carry any perks, but I found I wasn't singled out as much for ridicule. Or perhaps the *Super* didn't want to antagonise someone who was now taller and fitter than he was.

Generally speaking, the boys got on very well with each other but there were no concrete relationships, no one had a best friend, we all just got on. Playtime was on the lawn. In truth, this was the furthest thing imaginable from a lawn, although that was what we called it. It was about the size of half a football pitch and it was just compacted dirt, no grass at all. This area was Wembley and Lords all rolled into one for all of us. We re-created great footy matches of the time, usually whoever Leeds United were playing that week.

We also played many a test match with Geoff Boycott batting and Fred Trueman bowling. Many a World Cup victory was won on the lawn, and it really helped, let me tell you when England won the actual World Cup in 1966.

We lived off that game for months. I captained the winning side against the Germans - it was only 7-a-side but what a game. We re-lived it over and over again. It was times like this that made living in care bearable. We were all like-minded souls looking to escape, even if only for a few hours. Once we were back inside, it was yes miss, yes *Matron*, yes *Super*, sorry miss, and so on.

Miss Mary Weatherall and pictured right on a camel while leading an educational trip to Egypt in December 1968

There was one creature that loved the boys and was very free with its cuddles. He was Sooty the cat. Sooty was there when I arrived, a formidable Tom cat, jet black and about the size of a small terrier. He was a bit of a warrior when he went out, often coming back with his ear torn or a bit of fur missing but he loved to cuddle up on someone's lap when we were watching television.

He would often avoid the front of the room where the best, biggest and softest seats were, instead jumping up on the lap of one of the boys to curl up and have a sleep. It was as if he was cocking a snoot to the staff *"If you lot don't give them a cuddle, I will."* Or maybe he purred words to that effect.

It was a sad day when we all realised no one had seen Sooty for a few days. This wasn't unusual as he would often not come in after a night on the tiles but like I said, he hadn't been seen for a few days. It was *Matron* who raised the alarm and asked us all to go out and see if we could find him. We drew a blank. He was nowhere to be found.

It was me who found him a couple of days later. I was on shoe cleaning duty by myself in the cloakroom. I had always been aware of the shoe rack not butting up to the wall but had never really thought about it. There was a gap of about six inches behind the rack that half-filled the wall. This was because part of the central heating system ran round the back of it, a warm place I thought, as I polished my umpteenth black shoe.

I looked behind as best I could, but it was too dark. I fetched the torch that was always by the back door in case anyone had to go outside after dark. Shining the light behind the shoe rack, there he was, curled up tight in the far corner, facing the wall. The old boy must have taken himself in there to pass away peacefully.

I told *Matron* I had found him and the situation he was in. I needed a few of the boys to help me move the shoe rack away from the wall. *Matron* wanted him to be buried in the rose garden that was overlooked by the office window. I volunteered to take care of it and with dignity and tears in my eyes, I dug his little grave, wrapped him in a large towel given to me for that specific reason and laid Sooty to rest.

When I got back to school, I had a special favour to ask Mr *Dewey Dew Drop* Dewhirst, our woodwork teacher. *"Sir, we lost our cat at the home, can I please make a small wooden cross to put over his grave."* Permission was granted and I fashioned the cross out of two pieces of oak and topped it off by burning his name along the cross section. I would often glance across to the rose garden whenever I was on my way up to the lawn, where Sooty's cross stood tall and proud.

By the time of the World Cup victory in 1966, I had settled into life in care. The passage of time flows very swiftly and is a great healer for young minds. My family were a distant memory, I no longer thought about them all, but my mother was never far from my thoughts.

My initial feelings of loss and solitude and the nights I cried myself to sleep with her being the last thought before I succumbed to Morpheus had now been replaced with thoughts of insecurity. The tears had stopped flowing and I was now asking myself, why? Did my mother not love me? Why did she leave me? Why had all those bad things happened to me? Of course, I could never find the answers to these questions but it's strange how my outlook had changed. I was beginning to become hardened and bitter as the realisation was dawning on me that I was on my own.

I found out many years later that my sister Kathleen had got married in 1966 and my brother David had given her away – 11 miles from where I was living in the children's home. It was revelations like these, years after I thought my nightmare had ended, that brought all those memories flooding back. Those feelings of being alone were still with me, I was right back in that children's home, and I would be uncared for and unloved.

I did go on my holiday to Cleethorpes, but it wasn't as much fun as I thought a holiday should be. Going to the seaside with about a dozen children and four members of staff wasn't the best recipe for a good time, particularly for the older boys who would feel embarrassed to be herded about the town. No one was allowed to go out on their own, always with a member of staff.

A couple of years later, I was to be the first boy to smash this rule and do my own thing. It wasn't too bad for the younger ones who loved to go to the open-air Lido and were always straight into the water, the cold, cold water. Once was enough for me. I preferred my swimming in the warm tropical climate of the Red Sea so anything after that was a poor second. I did go in for a swim during my first Cleethorpes holiday. I turned blue, got goose bumps and wrapped up in a massive towel provided by the guest house. I made sure I never went close to the Lido water again. We didn't go with a full complement of boys to Cleethorpes as those who were able to go home for a week did so. This was something that never arose for me nor for a few of my friends.

The amusement arcades were the places we would head for, our pockets weighed down with coppers for the machines. We thought we were rich when we were on holiday. Each of us had a gift from the organisation (council) that ran the home, a cash sum depending on your age.

The older you were, the more money you were given but it was never a fortune. This was looked after by a member of staff and distributed a bit at a time as and when asked for. We didn't always get it. If the *Super* thought you were spending your money in a silly way, your request was refused. This gift was also brought into play all year round and it would be used to punish any bad behaviour. If someone didn't do their duty properly, got into trouble or fighting, a fine of threepence or a sixpence was entered into a book and just before the holiday, the running total was deducted from their holiday money.

There was a way to boost your holiday cash though but that involved saving your pocket money. We didn't get much and the thought of handing some of it back was hard to justify.

Just before my first Christmas in the children's home, there was a spate of petty thefts. Nothing major but some of the boys would have a toy or money taken from their private drawers next to the bed. There were no locks on the drawers and they were open to anybody who cared to have a look inside.

I didn't have any personal toys or anything that could be considered valuable and any money I had on a Saturday morning was pretty much spent that same day, either over at Hollybrook Guest House on sweets, or on a trip down into Ilkley and maybe a knickerbocker glory in the Continental café at the bottom of Wells Road.

Miss Green and Miss Copeland were trying to find the culprit. Accusations were bandied about, and people were wrongly accused. There were many arguments and still the thief went undetected.

In my time at *Hill Top*, stealing was never an issue other than a few sweets but this incident went on for several weeks. It wasn't only the drawers that were targeted but school bags and coats that were hung up in the cloakroom were also game for the thief's attention.

It was only a matter of time before the culprit was found as the staff were beginning to adapt a more softly softly approach. They had their suspicions I am sure, but for now they were being played close to their chests. On a few occasions, they were busted going through our personal drawers but to be fair, their motive was to try and find the stolen items without resorting to any false accusations.

The conclusion to this one-man crime wave came to an unexpected end on a Saturday morning when we were up on the lawn kicking the ball about. The ball disappeared over the fence into the out-of-bounds area. One of the youngsters scurried after it, nipping under the wire and disappearing into the bushes. Two minutes later, he reappeared, minus the ball but with a handful of toys.

It was no wonder the staff couldn't find the stolen toys and treasure as they were stashed outside in the no-go area. *"Look at this lot,"* said the young lad, *"And there's loads more stuff down there as well."*

We all trailed down and found the hidden booty underneath some broken branches and piles of leaves. Collecting it all up, some of the boys carried it triumphantly back down to the home and straight to *Super's* office.

The news had gone round like wildfire and all the boys living in the home were eagerly waiting to get their stuff back, and they did, but the culprit was never unmasked. It was clear we had a master burglar in our midst, one who knew how to cover his tracks and avoid detection.

That evening the *Super* got us all together and asked for the thief to own up, *"Nothing will be done,"* he said, *"Everyone has their things back so own up and it will be forgotten."* No one was forthcoming, no one was so stupid. I knew as did all the lads that if *Super* got his hands on the thief, he wouldn't be able to sit down for a week.

Saturday mornings after breakfast, when we had done our tasks, was pocket money parade. This took place in the dining room on the long table under the window, the table where the staff sat.

On the left sat *Matron*, next to her was the *Super* and on the right was one of the staff. *Matron* would call your name and how much pocket money you were entitled to less any fines for bad behaviour. Sometimes, if you had been very naughty, your pocket money was suspended completely. This would only happen when there was any unacceptable behaviour such as absconding or nicking off.

You would go forward where the *Super* was counting out your cash and collect it. If you wanted to save any for your holiday, you would then move on to the staff member and give whatever you wanted to save to her. After the pocket money parade, we were taken in groups across the road to the Hollybrook Guest House where the owner, Mr Spiers, would let us buy sweets and chocolate bars.

The older boys were allowed to take a walk down into Ilkley on Saturdays. This wasn't as popular as you might think. When we were about the town, we always felt so conspicuous as the clothes we wore made us stand out like a sore thumb. It was the shirt collars mostly. They had been washed and ironed so many times that they were like pieces of paper that would flap around with no semblance of stiffness at all.

Rightly or wrongly, local people were a little suspicious of the boys. To some extent, we had to suffer bad press because we lived just a couple of hundred yards from an approved school, Moorlands House (much like a borstal) and as such were treated with suspicion in the same way.

It angers me to this day when I see postings on forum groups that say my children's home, *Hill Top* *"was a home for naughty boys."* It most certainly was not. The majority of souls that ended up in care in Ilkley were from broken homes where they weren't looked after properly or because there was a sudden change in family circumstance.

The list of reasons for boys being in care was endless

Having said that, there was also a boy I remember who was brought to the home because his parents couldn't control him. He had been in trouble with the police but was always cautioned and taken back home. I suppose the judge on his last appearance at the children's panel thought a short sharp shock was needed so he was sent to *Hill Top*, which was seen as a lesser punishment than going to the approved school.

I remember he carried on with his shenanigans and would run away at every opportunity. There was one instance when he committed a crime while away on the run and he was caught red-handed in the kitchen of a house, his pockets stuffed with fruit of all things, but he had also nicked some jewellery. We were simply told that he would not be returning. I saw him a few months later cleaning the gardens up the road in Moorlands House, so no more freedom for him.

The Christmas holidays were upon us. School had broken up and quite a few of the lads had gone back home for the festive season leaving just eight of us for my second Christmas in care. I used to love Christmas, my mother and father would play tricks all Christmas day by asking me to go for this or go fetch that and when I did, I would find another present that had been hidden previously.

My past Christmases with my family were all good memories, with swimming and fishing, camel riding, family fun and friends always coming round. But since my mother's death and I found it hard to lift myself out of my self-imposed mental flagellation. Christmas and 31st December is still a dates that find me cold and distant at times, lost in my own world.

But that said, if ever there was a time when *Hill Top* was bearable, it was Christmas Day. With most of the lads away, the staff seemed so much more agreeable, punishments were often overlooked and the boundaries for certain things were stretched a little allowing our confidence to grow knowing we had more leeway.

A couple of the younger lads would busy themselves making presents for the staff, nothing major, usually a card or the like. The day itself would start as normal, up to the bathroom for a strip wash, dressed and down for breakfast. This was the most casual day of the year, and the lads could chat away without fear of reprisals. There was also the odd outburst of laughter, a good start to the day.

We still had the chores to do after breakfast, kitchen duties etc but after that it was all into the television room where the *Super* had a couple of big sacks. The television was on showing the Christmas morning programmes featuring the popular Lesley Crowther as he toured the children's hospital.

The *Super* would pull out a present (they were from the council run social services department) and call your name to go and collect it. The lads would then disappear to all points of the home as they played with their new toy. There were no other duties that day other than down in the kitchen after meals. We were free to do what we liked, go for a walk on the moors, make snowmen if the snow god had been kind, or just sit and read.

The atmosphere changed overnight. Christmas was over for another year and Boxing Day was seen more for the adults than the children. There was a marked change in the *Super*, *Matron* and the staff, almost as if they were somehow pleased that they could stop trying to be friendly and get on with normality.

But it didn't help my mental state as we got nearer to New Year's Eve. The closer it came I would shrink more and more into myself, cutting myself off from my surroundings. At this time, I spoke very infrequently, lost in my own thoughts.

I knew it was impossible, but I used to wish and pray that mum would turn up and take me away reassuring me that everything would be fine, saying it was all a dream, *"Come on Pete, we're going back to Aden,"* but it never happened, and life went on.

The boys who had been fortunate enough to get away for Christmas started to come back, the return spread out over several days, with one or two not coming back until the New Year.

With Christmas behind us, the next high point of my year was the summer holiday and after that, Christmas again.

This was the seasonal repetition of life at *Hill Top*.

Chapter Seven

The Elland Road Terraces

The weekends in care were the hardest to bear. Most of the children would have family visit them and they would take them down into Ilkley for the afternoon and some would stay in the home with their visitors, usually in the dining room or up on the lawn for a kick-about. For those of us who had no visitors, it was just another day without school.

One practice that was forever unfair was the confiscation of goods and sweets that were left after family visits. This was to ensure no other child felt left out when those around him were scoffing chocolate or playing with a new toy.

I remember one of my pals, Tony. After his mother left, he had a massive package of sweets, every sort you could wish for and enough to keep him in clover for the rest of the week. The *Super* called him into the office with his stash and he reappeared after a few minutes, tears in his eyes and clutching a single bar of chocolate.

To be fair, he should have known the drill as all excess sweets were taken away for the reason mentioned above. But there was one saving grace. Every so often, for a treat when there was a good film on the telly, out would come this confiscated contraband and everyone would get a dip-in.

But telly time was a chore, possibly the worst time of the day for me. The sitting room was divided into two. On the left was an area for quiet reading and board games, which also doubled as the place where the staff did the ironing; and on the right, there was the television in the far corner which faced out into the room with three rows of seven hard seats at the back of the room and a couch and three armchairs at the front.

The front area was comfy and relaxing but was reserved for the *Super*, *Matron* and staff. I had the misfortune of not being able to whisper very efficiently, and consequently I was always getting into trouble for talking through a film. The *Super* was so fed up with me one night, I was despatched off to my bed without supper. It was a lousy film anyway.

For me, school was my go-to place where my classmates accepted me for who I was, not where I came from. This is where my firm friends were but unfortunately these were term time friendships and would end on my way home from school. Actually getting to school from the home was a daily route march and took the best part of an hour – both ways.

The day would start with one of the live-in staff going from bedroom to bedroom at five-minute intervals from 7am getting us all up. Then straight to the bathroom where we came immediately under the supervision of the *Super*, sat on his chair in the corner, back to the wall, arms across the back rest. It was never the best way to start the day. I detested his presence in the bathroom. This seemed to be his favourite place and he would take a lot of pleasure in finding new ways to ridicule us all. To make matters worse, some of his favourites would join in with the mickey taking, giving him extra credence and for those who were laughing, a sense of being on his side.

After the morning strip wash and teeth brushing, it was back to the bedroom to make your bed. It had to be made to an exact science. If it was done in a hurry and looked untidy, you would come back after school and find the complete bundle of bedding including sheets in a pile on the floor ready for you to do the job properly all over again.

With beds made and everyone dressed, it was down to the dining room for breakfast. There were dozens of boxes of small, individual cereal packets and you picked your favourite, emptied it into a dish and the milk was waiting at the table in a big jug.

Some of the younger children would have a problem lifting and pouring the jug of milk properly. I was invariably the table monitor and would gladly help them. I wasn't charged with doing so but to leave them to their own devices would invite a calamity and retribution from the staff. As with all our meals, they were eaten in silence unless the *Super* spoke to someone. If he did, this was the signal for all of us to have a few words under our breath to our immediate neighbour, but we dared not utter too loudly, and in any event, we were silenced very quickly.

Breakfast was a simple affair. Toast was ever present and sometimes strawberry jam appeared on the dumb waiter that appeared as if by magic from the kitchen directly below. And we all enjoyed a glass of milk.

When we were on kitchen duty and after our meals, we would take it in turns to work the dumb waiter. Those on dining room duty would load the dirty dishes onto it, then on a signal, usually *"Okay"* bellowed at the top of their voice, it was lowered out of sight to be collected by the kitchen brigade down below. The meals were delivered in the same way but were placed on the dumb waiter by the cook, a nice lady although we didn't get much exposure to her or her helper, only straight after meals when those on kitchen duty would go and clean the kitchen and do the washing up. One of the live-in staff was always there to supervise so talking and getting to know the staff who came in each day was never practical.

Breakfast was the only time we were excused kitchen duties on a school day, simply because we didn't have enough time. From the table, we would go through to the cloakroom where everyone's shoes were placed in a massive shoe rack that took over one half of a complete wall. The rack was about six feet long and six feet high with dozens of compartments. The rack was a series of boxes and reminded me of the type that you saw in the reception of a hotel with letters in. But our shoe rack was so much bigger!

There were also dozens of coat pegs, each with the name of the occupant written above. Beyond the shoe rack were three toilet cubicles. The last cubicle was adjacent to the door that led to the outside, this door was our way of leaving and entering the children's home. Although there were other external doors - there was one direct into the kitchen below and the front door at the side of the *Super's* office - both of these doors were out of bounds to the children, as was the front garden underneath the window of the office.

The shoes were always cleaned and ready for us, courtesy of the shoe brigade. As with all the jobs we had to do at *Hill Top,* there was a rota and two boys each evening would spend up to two hours cleaning and polishing all the school shoes, as many as 18 pairs. We would do this for a week at a time, sitting on the floor and like everything else that we were tasked to do, the completed shoes had to be checked by a member of staff. If one shoe was not up to scratch, they all had to be done again.

I soon wised up to a few shortcuts that we could use on most of our rotas. If any of my shoes failed the inspection, the rejects would be thrown onto the floor and the others would follow until the floor of the cloakroom was littered with shoes. We could never get them mixed up because our names were in them and also on each pigeon-hole.

When the rejects were dropped on the floor, I would casually move them into a small pile when no one was looking. Then when the rest of the shoes were thrown down, I had two separate piles, one pile had already been passed inspection so it followed they would be good again. Then the good ones were simply replaced so we could concentrate on the others.

One such evening after a shoe brigade inspection, I remember to this day with a smile on my face, two lads laughing and giggling after we had been allowed out to play up on the lawn.

I asked them what was so funny and they told me quite hysterically that the inspection of the shoes had failed and true to form, all were emptied on the floor. The two lads said to each other, *"Sod this for a fucking game of marbles"* and put them all back again, doing no further cleaning.

They sat on the floor chatting for about half an hour and then went to tell Miss that they had finished. She came, inspected a second time and passed the shoes. The lads thought it was hilarious and they gained massive respect that evening from the other lads. No one said anything to the staff, it was looked upon as a victory for us.

After breakfast we put our coats and school shoes on, and it was time to go to school. I would start to smile inwardly as I was going to be away from the children's home for the next nine hours or so.

I needed to be out of the home by 8am in order to get to the school on Valley Drive for 9.15am. Out onto Westwood Drive, cross the cattle grid and down the road and onto Wells Road which took me downhill all the way into Ilkley.

White Wells, just as Peter remembers it all those years ago

My first port of reference would be the College of Housecraft where I would always pause and try to spot a few fish in the great big ponds in the grounds of the college.

The moors were a picture in the summer and the heathers were a bright array of purple as far as the eye could see. White Wells, an old Roman bath, was always there to greet me every morning. I never tired of it and spent many happy hours during the holidays and weekends walking around the trails that criss-crossed this part of the moors.

Turning the bend further down the hill there was another cattle grid and a maternity home. From here, you could see all the way down Wells Road into the heart of Ilkley town. From *Hill Top* to the town seemed like many a mile, but in reality, it was no more than a solitary mile.

Going to school was the easy bit. Coming home was torture! That hill was massive. I would turn right at the bottom of Wells Road, past the Winter Gardens. There used to be a little sweet shop here and if I had any pocket money left over, I would nip in for a quarter of midget gems, the staple food for all the lads at the home.

I didn't normally walk with any of the other lads, I tried to get away quickly and be in front. I didn't like to be in a group as the boys in a group stood out. If I was on my own, I might not be noticed.

With my sweets in my pocket, I'd cross the road and go over the foot bridge that spans the railway line leading to Ilkley railway station. I would then head towards Valley Drive, and from there it was a straight walk to school.

A couple of my classmates lived on Valley Drive, and I would always call for them… Ian Crawford was first and then Peter Cockerill. The three of us were pretty much inseparable through our last two years at school. About 20 minutes later, we would arrive at school together, just in time to take our bags to the classroom then head to the hall for assembly.

In those days, school ended at 4.15pm, we had to be back in the home by 5.15pm. Most of the trip back to Hill Top along Valley Drive was done at a running pace so I could get to Wells Road in good time. After that no way could I or anyone for that matter, run up that hill.

Saturday morning was always cleaning day. We each had our bedroom duties to do. With between three and four boys to a room, one would be responsible for dusting, one would have to sweep the floor, one would wipe the woodwork and furniture with a clean, wet cloth.

When we had finished, one of us would go and fetch either the *Super* or one of the staff to come and inspect the room.

The inspection was meticulous. While each of us were made to stand with our hands behind our backs at the side of our bed, fingers were run over the skirting boards and window ledges looking for the slightest speck of dust. We each had a chest of drawers and these would be pulled out to make sure all was clean behind and the beds were pulled out in turn, again to make sure we had cleaned properly. If it didn't pass the inspection, and quite often it didn't, we had to do it all over again.

I remember on one occasion, the *Super* seemed to be in a particularly bad mood, talking to himself as he searched for dirt. He had a bad habit of talking to himself, the lads used to take the mickey out of him all of the time, but he never heard them.

We failed the inspection no less than four times, each time for something quite miniscule. One of the times we thought we had cracked it. The *Super* found no dirt at all until he came to the last two feet of skirting by the door. As he ran his fingers along it, he collected a minute amount of dust and his face lit up. He was almost purple by now with all the bending down but the look of triumph on his podgy face was unmistakable.

He had us all stand next to our our beds and as he passed each of us, showing us the dirt on his stubby, sausage-like fingers, inches from our faces, he uttered just three words as he left the room, *"Do it again."* The day was fast disappearing. The four of us had been hard at the cleaning all morning, even returning to continue after lunch. By the time we were able to get outside it was almost 3pm and the day was almost gone.

Meanwhile the World Cup victory of England over West Germany had brought a huge resurgence in football right across the country and *Hill Top* children's home was no exception.

Leeds United were the team of choice for everyone at the home thanks to one lad, Steve Little. Steve was a good lad and would pester the staff whenever he could into letting him go to a football match, but his pleading words fell on deaf ears - that is until his social worker came to see him one day.

Now, when your social worker came, it was always on a one-to-one basis, just you and them. Quite often you would go out for a walk or go for a game of something up on the lawn. This was your time to ask questions and get news from home.

Anyway, on this particular visit, Steve must have been asking why he couldn't go to watch his beloved Leeds United playing when they were at home. This was carried back to the care team for discussion. It came as a massive surprise one Friday at teatime when the *Super* said a few of the senior lads could go to a home game at Elland Road.

Steve Little was a hero. It was he who knew the ropes and where to go and we were happy for him to take the lead. We realised that if we messed this opportunity up, we would never be allowed to go again.

Three of us set off one Saturday morning after chores, taking the train from Ilkley to Leeds and then a bus to Elland Road.

This was amazing. I had never experienced anything like it in my life. I knew all the players, as each of us had played make-believe being them often enough up on the lawn.

Peter's favourite Peter Lorimer in action at Elland Road

Peter Lorimer was my favourite, then big Jack Charlton. We always went into the Kop, the covered North Stand end of the ground where all the noisiest home fans congregated.

The atmosphere was fantastic and had to be the best escape from being in care ever. Of course, we behaved ourselves, going straight to the ground and straight back after the game. We knew this was the only way to preserve our enjoyment and for us to be able to keep going to games.

I remember one game when Leeds were home to Liverpool, I secretly admired Liverpool FC and

England forward Roger Hunt was my personal hero. Somehow, for that game, we ended up right at the front of the stand, right behind the goal, I could have reached out and touched my heroes.

But I remembered the day more for increasing my vocabulary of swear words! There was this woman standing just behind, a big woman with a deep booming voice. She was immediately noticeable when she spoke but when she shouted, everyone within a 50-yard radius knew. She had more expletive words than I had ever heard before… and some of them I had no idea what they meant. But it was fun.

I turned round once when she uttered a long barrage of obscenities as Liverpool were on the attack. My mouth was wide open and eyes staring straight at her. She must have been amused because she ruffled my hair and winked at me. I liked her.

Then Liverpool got a corner. Roger Hunt came up into the box but before the ball was crossed, she had set her sights on him. *"Hunt, you fucking fanny, you blond headed bastard, you ain't nothing but a fucking great big scouser prick."* As she bellowed this out, I felt a hand on my shoulder and she gave me a friendly squeeze. I loved life on the terraces.

By the time we got back from a game on Saturday afternoon, the teatime meal was over, all done and dusted, dishes washed and put away. But for those of us who went to the game, we had sandwiches on a plate and some sort of pudding to follow.

At last, my life at *Hill Top* was beginning to look up and weekends were now something to look forward to… and even better things were beginning to happen.

Ilkley Cricket Club today with more modern infrastructure than in the 1960s

I played cricket at school during the summer terms. We only played friendlies and we never played in a school league or anything like it.

Our sports master, Mick Moore, thought I had a gift for the game and encouraged me to go along to Ilkley Cricket Club. Anything of this nature had to get the approval of the *Super*. I mentioned it to him one afternoon in the holidays and asked if I could go. I was pleasantly surprised by his answer, and off I went down Wells Road, through town, across the main road and over the river. I hardly stopped until I got to the ground.

I walked around minding my own business. There were no games on but lots of men were practising in the nets, and a few lads as well. *"Do you want to join in?"* asked one of the lads playing on an artificial wicket, *"You'll have to bowl a bit before you can have a bat though."* I didn't mind at all as bowling was my thing. I could bowl, and bowl well, I thought.

By this time, I stood a good six foot in height and although I still had a slender frame, I could turn my arm over quickly. I bowled a few down to the other lads, not really wanting to show off but I knew I could do better.

A bigger lad came into bat, *"Come on young 'un, show us what you got,"* he said. I obliged. I never needed a long run up - seven paces were all I used. I could generate a lot of power and speed through my shoulders and right arm. I had natural speed, it just needed honing.

The games we played at *Hill Top* were one-sided if I bowled. Most the boys simply could not stand the pace, so all my games up there were limited to me bowling spinners.

I came into my delivery stride and let rip. The ball pitched on a good length, left the batsman stranded in mid shot, continued past his chest and carried on clearing the keeper's outstretched hands and on to the boundary. *"Fucking hell!"* he shouted, *"What the bloody hell was that?"*

"You wanted to see what I had, that was it," I replied. I was 14 years old and beginning to grow into myself, making my way in life and for the first time had an interest outside the children's home. It was as if Ilkley was showing approval and accepting me.

I was asked to join in with the men that same evening. There were two squads practising, the first team and the second team. They both played in the Aire Wharfedale Cricket League. I joined the second team in their practice session and was enjoying the attention they paid to me, and they let me bowl. Me, 14 years old, bowling at and playing cricket with grown men! I noticed that the younger lads had packed up now and were sitting on the grass watching.

After practice, the skipper called me into the pavilion for a talk. He wanted to know who I was and if I would like to join the club. I was very excited, if not a little guarded and went on to explain I was from a children's home nearby and the superintendent would have to give me permission to join.

The skipper told me to leave it to him and he would make enquiries. He told me that the next full practice was on Tuesday evening, starting at 6.30pm and that I was most welcome to come down.

It was one Monday after school that the *Super* called me into the office. He told me that one of the officials from the Ilkley Cricket Club had been in touch asking if I could join the club with a view to playing regular Sunday mornings with the junior team and the odd Saturday afternoon if selected to play for the second team. I was granted permission and my association with proper cricket had begun.

The coaches at Ilkley were brilliant. They worked with me, helping me to develop as a bowler and all the time I was getting lots of games with the juniors which gave me a massive boost in confidence.

Halfway through the season, I received a post card in the mail, addressed to me and delivered to the home. I had been selected to play for the second team that Saturday. To say I was over the moon was an understatement. The *Super* seemed to be genuinely pleased as well, and he told me there had never been a boy from his home that had played representative sport.

I was in a dream throughout the day of my debut for Ilkley seconds, I remember it so vividly even after all these years. The visitors won the toss and chose to bat.

We were fielding and half way into the innings I was brought into the attack. The skipper consulted me like any of his other bowlers, asking me what kind of field I wanted, and if I wanted anyone in close. I was on the verge of bursting, 14 years old and setting my own field in league cricket!

I took two wickets that innings, it was the best day of my life.

The selection cards came in the post on a regular basis after that. Towards the end of the season, I was thrown the new ball at the start of the innings and the skipper asked me to open the bowling.

I couldn't believe it. After the game, some of the older blokes came up to me and congratulated me. They weren't sure but they thought I had just broken the record for being the youngest opening bowler in the League. I was still only 14 years and five months old. My spell at Ilkley Cricket Club lasted as long as I was at the home and my love for the game is as strong in my retirement as it ever has been.

Chapter Eight

Bullying and Gardens

There were a couple of pairs of brothers at Hill Top and one set of three as well. But the oldest of this trio left soon after I arrived. He was older than me and it was time for him to move on.

This was the way of things when in care, I noticed it a few times and was very apprehensive for when it was to be my time.

Each of us had a social worker and mine was Mr Watson. I saw Mr Watson on a few occasions at *Hill Top* and each time I thought he was coming to see me, but it would be some other boy. The social worker would see if there was any chance you could fit back into family life if you were an age to earn a living. Then plan B would be to find you a flat and where possible, a job as well. The first thing would be to get accommodation in place, a job would be secondary.

When the great day arrived, there was no ceremony, no fond farewell from the staff… to them it was just another day. But to you, it was the most important day of your life up to that point. It was the day you would either sink or swim. It was that clear cut.

I remember vividly the eldest of the trio of brothers leaving. He was sat in *Super's* office with a small case waiting for his social worker to collect him. In his case were packed most of the clothes he had acquired, plus one or two personal effects, but he had given most of his belongings to his brothers.

For most of the morning, he sat on his own while the *Super* and *Matron* were going about their own business. It didn't cross their minds to sit with the lad to offer advice or any other bits of knowledge that he could take away with him. His social worker came and didn't even come into the home. The *Super* called the lad and walked with him to the car.

His brothers were unaware of this development as they were playing up on the lawn and none of the staff thought to fetch them so they could say goodbye to their older brother. Without any fuss other than the *Super* being present to say goodbye, the lad got into the car and was driven away. I never saw him again and trust he made his way in the world as he would have wanted to.

There may have been mitigating circumstances that prevented a warm goodbye from his siblings, I had no way of knowing, but what I do know is that both the brothers were heartbroken for the rest of the day.

The staff of the home were conspicuous by their absence, but this attitude of non-caring, no compassion was witnessed time and time again during my time at the children's home. The younger brother of the trio, I'll call him Christopher, was to feature quite alarmingly later on that year in what I term to be the darkest days in the home.

Generally speaking, bullies didn't get much of a foothold at *Hill Top*. One or two tried to influence some of the other boys but it was pretty much short-lived when they realised the boys on a whole were a strong bunch when united.

Like everything in life, there are always exceptions and this lad, William, 13 years old, was just that. He came to us halfway through the summer holidays when I was in my second year at *Hill Top*.

William had a distrust of everyone, a legacy of the way he had been living. He was the youngest of his family and endured a life at the bottom of the pecking order. Being a young teenager, William naturally gravitated towards the company of the older boys, myself included. But it was thought among my peer group that he was a bit of an idiot, fanciful and not averse to lying to get a point across. From what he told us in the first few days, his older brothers would often make his life a misery, thinking nothing of punching him and stealing anything he had of value.

At first, he was quite vocal. He had a captive audience and enjoyed telling the other lads how he was the *cock of the walk* where he came from. William's stories were pure fantasy, but the younger lads lapped it up.

With his new-found group of younger lads, William drifted away quite quickly from the older group to become a big fish in a little pond with the youngsters. It wasn't too long before he started to get demonstrative, acting out his stories of violence on some of the other lads who were in no position to respond. The stories got more and more fanciful. William was now realising he was no longer the bottom of the pecking order but in the little group he created, he was now top dog.

William's time at the home was drawing to a close because his behaviour was spiralling out of control and his actions towards the young ones were becoming almost tyrannical. It was time for the older boys to have a word, but it was a situation that didn't go to plan.

We older boys got William on his own up on the lawn. We told him he was out of order as on more than one occasion he had punched lads for no other reason than to demonstrate what he claimed he used to do to others when he was at home.

William felt threatened by this confrontation with older boys and to some extent it must have dredged up memories of back home at the hands of his older brothers. Bolstered by his recent episodes of bravado, William hit out unexpectedly and hit out hard, catching our friend Tony squarely on the point of his chin, dropping him like a stone.

"Do you want some?" urged William, looking directly at me, *"I'll do the pair of you."* He threw a punch, but I grabbed his arm and at the same time Stewart grabbed him round the neck and the pair of us wrestled him to the ground and held him there.

With the situation under control, we realised Tony was still flat on his back and unconscious. Grabbing hold of William's arms, we pulled him to his feet as Tony began to move and roll around the floor. *"You okay Tony?"* I asked, *"I'm fine… but fuck it hurts,"* he added, rubbing his chin.

He got up off the floor, looked straight at William. He was now in control, and started towards him. His lips curling up *"You fucking bastard, let's see how you get on when I'm ready for you."*

Putting my hand out I said *"No, go and get cleaned up, leave this to us."*

We were now in a quandary. It wasn't the done thing to go to the *Super*, as it went against the code of *them and us*. Instead, we pushed him up against the green wire fence that encircled the lawn.

The three of us were breathing heavily after our little skirmish. Stewart and I started to tell him that he was well out of order in the way he lorded it over the other lads with his systematic bullying. All we got in return was *"Fuck off, fuck the lot of you."* At that,

William forced himself forward, pushing both me and Stewart aside and headed down to the home. We followed, not wanting to escalate the conflict but to satisfy us that no one else was going to feel the brunt of William's almost feral anger.

There were three of the younger lads in the cloakroom when William arrived and not saying a word, he set about punching and kicking them. The lads were screaming for help.

Stewart and I were a matter of yards behind on the path but by the time we got to the cloakroom door, all three were squirming on the floor, bruised and bloodied. Stewart ran at William grabbing him by the arms and getting him to the ground, where punches were thrown. On a one-to-one, William wasn't the fighter he thought he was. Stewart battered him to the point where I intervened and pulled him off leaving William in a heap, crying like a baby.

All this occurred in a matter of seconds. By the time I intervened, the *Super* and the staff were racing through the dining room. At first glance it looked like a straightforward fight between Stewart and William but when the three other lads told their story, and I filled in the gaps, the whole situation of the preceding 10 minutes was revealed.

The police were called, and William was taken away. The *Super* told us later that he was charged and would not be returning to the home. In total, William had been with us about two weeks, but he certainly left his mark.

Sunday was always a quiet day. After breakfast we would go and put our Sunday best on for church parade. Walking two abreast, crocodile fashion, we made our way down the never-ending hill to St Margaret's Church.

St Margaret's Church in Ilkley

This was an imposing building. I knew nothing of architecture, gargoyles and flying buttresses, but it looked magnificent.

Steps up to the massive oak door led you inside to a large gathering place before going on into the heart of the church. As a group, we had our own set of pews where we would sit, stand and kneel with a little bit of singing in between.

The vicar was a huge chap. I remember thinking his gowns would look more at home strapped to the mast of a sailing ship. We were primed by the *Super* to have some coppers in our pockets so we could contribute to the collection plate. Some of us lads mastered the art of making a lot of noise when we put our pennies into the plate giving the impression we were contributing more than we actually were.

On one particular Sunday when the service was finished, we were waiting in our pews for the church to empty. As normal, the vicar would greet each one of us as we passed him at the door, the *Super* standing at his side.

This morning, when I was just passing the vicar, the *Super* spoke out, *"This is young Foster,"* he said to the vicar, who took hold of my hand and shook it as if he was ringing a hand bell. He told me that one of his elderly parishioners was struggling with her garden and would really like some help at the weekend.

I looked at the *Super*, and it was clear he was already appraised of the situation and he nodded. I remember blurting out something along the lines of *"Yes sir, of course I would like to help the lady, where does she live?"*

"Don't worry about the details just yet," said the vicar, *"Your superintendent has all the details and he will sort it for*

you, thank you for your kindness, you are a credit, god bless you."

We set off back up the hill to the home. Just by the maternity home on the left-hand side going up Wells Road, the *Super* stopped our procession and came to me pointing across the road to the junction of Wells Road with Crossbeck Road, explaining: *"This is where the old lady lives, I'll bring you back down later today to introduce you."*

Sunday dinner was one of the best meals of the week. We could have fruit juice or lemonade with our meal and the pudding was usually something a little special. Arctic roll was a firm favourite.

Being one of the older boys by this time, it would usually fall to me to be part of the kitchen duty but not so this day. The *Super* and I set off after dinner to walk down Wells Road to meet the lady I had volunteered to help.

I didn't enjoy my time in the *Super's* company. His habit of talking to himself under his breath was strange and made me nervous.

As we turned off Wells Road, we passed the maternity home and started to walk along Crossbeck Road. The houses were set well back from the road and looked imposing. They were all terraced and on three floors with each gateway at the top of a flight of stone steps.

From the pavement outside the elderly lady's house, we were met with eight stone steps and a wall on either side. Each side of the wall was decorated with black ornamental handrails. The top step levelled out onto a flagged area about three feet square with a footpath running up the side all the way to the front door, some 30 feet distant.

First impressions assured me she was a very nice lady and quite clearly with mobility problems. She was of a slight build with grey hair and I remember her shoulders were hunched over and she walked with a stoop aided by a walking stick. She had a very small pair of spectacles perched on her nose with a black cord attached. I was introduced to her as *"Peter."* This would have been one of only a handful of times in all my time at the home that the *Super* had used my Christian name in my presence.

Mrs Poole was the lady's name, and we sat and talked for about 45 minutes over a cup of tea and some biscuits. It was mostly the *Super* who did the talking but eventually Mrs Poole and I began to chat together. She was funny at times and because of her years, I would guess late 70s to early 80s, she would also seem to forget what we were talking about.

On my way in I noticed the garden which was severely neglected and needed a lot of hard work, mainly digging and weeding. The weeds were everywhere. The introduction and pleasantries came to an end with the *Super* asking Mrs Poole if she felt I would do to help her in the garden on a Saturday morning. She was thrilled that at last she was getting some help. I was thrilled as well, it got me out of bedroom duty!

It was arranged that I would come down each Saturday morning for 10am and stay until 2 or 3pm.

I couldn't wait. The week dragged by but eventually next Saturday came around and after breakfast when my dormitory pals were getting ready for the cleaning, I was off, whistling my way down to see Mrs Poole.

My Saturdays had taken on a different meaning as I now had a purpose. Of course, during the cricket season, I would arrange to go earlier so that I could get away for around 12.30pm in time for me to get to the cricket ground.

The morning would usually start with a cup of coffee and some cake. I very quickly realised that Mrs Poole valued my company just as much as my ability to dig and weed her garden. Many is the time I would have to make an excuse that this, that or the other was needing doing this morning and then I would head out to the garden.

My upbringing around adults was very much old school as my parents would forever be saying, *"Children should be seen and not heard."* I followed these instructions religiously and added one of my own, to respect my elders. Just as I behaved in Miss Weatherall's company, so I did with Mrs Poole.

The work was hard as the garden had been neglected for several years but after the first three visits, we began to see the fruits of my labours.

There were two long flower beds on each side of the garden of approximately 30 feet in length from the top of the steps up to the front of the building. A path ran parallel to one bed with a mixture of rose and shrub beds interspaced to the other side of the path in the main body of the garden.

Before I was due to leave, Mrs Poole would call me in for a cup of tea or coffee, biscuits and cake. We would have a little chat for 15 minutes while I told her what I had done that morning and she would ask me if there was anything I needed for the next time.

We then had a little ritual that was enacted out after every visit. It went back to my first day with her. When I was leaving, she pressed a half-a-crown piece into my hand. I was taken by surprise and told her I was with her to help and I wanted no reward other than to see the garden improve on a regular basis. I smiled very politely, thanked her and gave her the coin back. She took it, gave me a little smile and reached for my jacket to pass to me. I thanked her for her hospitality and told her I would call again next Saturday, bidding her good day.

As I rounded the maternity home, crossing the cattle grid, I put my hand in my jacket pocket. I could feel something round and hard, there it was, a half-a-crown piece. A great big grin spread out over my face as I picked up my pace into a skip and flipped the coin with my thumb to catch it again and again.

Each visit after that, Mrs Poole would hand me my jacket, patting the pocket with a knowing smile and I swear one day she winked as well.

My last winter at *Hill Top* was a sad time when I learned from the *Super* that Mrs Poole had passed away. I had been her gardener for almost a full year, but in all that time I never saw any visitors, nor did she mention any family. I still find myself occasionally thinking of Mrs Poole when I see an overgrown garden. I was pleased and thankful to have been her friend.

Chapter Nine
Breaking the Mould

I was growing up quickly in the children's home. The staff, including the *Super* and *Matron*, for reasons known only to them, seemed to afford me a little more leeway than I had previously been subject to.

With hindsight, the change became noticeable after I started to play cricket for Ilkley. I wouldn't go as far as to say I was gaining respect from the figures in authority, but I would like to think I had their trust. As I entered my 5th year at school, I had never been in trouble other than being sent off to bed early. I had lost count of the number of times I was the subject of ridicule from the staff though, but I would never retaliate either by answering back or leaving the room, I would just fix a cold, unemotional stare in the direction of the perpetrator. My instincts told me this was the best form of defence.

The annual holiday to Cleethorpes was a couple of weeks away. It was the summer of 1968 and by this time, I was a strapping lad of 16 years. With a couple of not so exciting holidays already under my belt, the thought of a week at the seaside had lost its appeal, but as I had nowhere else to go, I would be the first on the list. A few of lads had gone home to spend a bit of time with their families, leaving the rest of us to pick up the slack on our regular cleaning rotas. But in general, it was a time for us to relax and get out on the moors around Ilkley. Privileges like this were earned and not given. Any form of misbehaviour like answering back to staff or not doing your jobs properly meant you were destined to spend your time on the lawn or in the games room.

I would spend all day rambling around White Wells and playing up on the Cow and Calf, a famous rock formation overlooking Ilkley town.

The closer we got to the holiday, the more my trips were restricted. I had to spend more time getting things ready and helping some of the younger lads to get their stuff together as well. Clothes were selected for the holiday, though we didn't have a big selection to choose from. If it didn't fit in the suitcase, it didn't go!

Bang on time, the coach would arrive to take us all to Cleethorpes, and the same guest house year after year. While we were in the guest house, discipline was paramount: no running, no swearing, no arguing and we all had to be on our best behaviour.

The first excitement after we arrived was a walk along the sea front. Walking in some form of orderly fashion, though not necessarily in columns of two, we looked exactly like what we were - a children's home on holiday, and this is what made it uncomfortable for me. The stigma of being in care was never going to go away. It couldn't be hidden, the only escape

from this was when I was with my teacher Miss
Weatherall or playing cricket.

Cleethorpes seaside resort in the 1960s

Things were to change however… never before
had any boys been able to go off on their own
without being accompanied by a member of staff.

The guest house we were staying in was a pleasant
place. The lady of the house was used to us and
always had a pleasant word or two to say. On this
particular holiday I was made aware that there was
some fishing tackle in the shed. Fishing was a
particular hobby of mine but for the last three years I
had been unable to go fishing.

On our travels around the seaside town, I noticed
a small pond about a mile from our guest house and
enquiries told me it was free fishing but there were

only small roach and perch in it. I very rarely approached the *Super* and almost never to ask for anything. But the holiday spirit was with me and the sea air made me a little light headed so I picked my moment.

"Super, can I go fishing please? There's a small pond down the road and the lady of the house told me I could borrow some tackle," I asked politely.

I was taken aback when he replied: *"When do you want to go?"*

"Tomorrow, if that's alright, please," I quickly responded. It was done. I had broken the shackles. I was on holiday and free to do my own thing... as long as it involved fishing.

I borrowed a garden fork and as a thank you, I volunteered to do some weeding in the garden of the guest house, which was handy because that's where the worms were... my chosen fishing bait.

I set off after breakfast, a packed lunch in my rucksack along with a reel and some hooks, floats and lead shot and so on. I carried the rod in my hands. It wasn't the best tackle I had seen but it served a purpose and if it let me get my bait in the water, it was good enough for me.

I made my way to the pond in double quick time. The sun was shining and there was hardly any wind, it was indeed a marvellous day. As for the fish, they must have been on their holidays as well. I caught nothing, but it was still the best day of the holidays for me.

I arrived back at the guest house just in time for tea. Having been sat in the sun all day, I had acquired a good dose of sunburn, and it was starting to get a little sore. I was given some lotion to put on my arms and face. That took the sting out the burn. It cooled me down and I was fine.

The *Super* started quizzing me about not catching any fish and at one point intimated that I hadn't been fishing at all. My answers must have satisfied him because I was allowed to go again the following day. The result was the same, no fish. I decided to pack up after lunch and take a slow walk back to the guest house. Leaving the pond, I crossed over the road and onto the beach, heading back towards the town.

There must have been some sea anglers fishing there recently. I began to find fresh flounder at the tide line. These were the fish that would have been returned after being caught and were washed back up onto the beach. Fresh fish I thought, he won't take the mickey out of me tonight! I had no idea how long the flounder were on the beach, but my instinct told me not very long.

They were supple, had both eyes (not yet attacked by gulls) and smelled fresh. With all boxes ticked, I gathered five of them and took them back to the guest house.

As I got nearer the town, I passed two anglers fishing in the sea, probably the two who caught my fish. Back at the guest house, I proudly showed off my catch, saying I had decided to fish in the sea today as the pond was no good. There was lots of admiration from the lads and the good lady of the house took the fish and was more than happy to cook them and serve them up for our tea. I never told anyone how I had really come by the fish. I was allowed to go off on my own fishing, and that is what I did.

A regular occurrence for children in the care system was *nicking off* or running away. I must have witnessed dozens of such actions and all bar one resulted in the boy or boys being returned either by parents, social workers or police. The one who didn't return took up lodgings further up the road at the approved school.

Generally, it was the younger lads that took flight. The most vulnerable ones. The ones who needed a little care, compassion and understanding - all three ingredients that were in short supply at *Hill Top*. Usually, the flight lasted just one night and for some of the lads, this was mission accomplished. They got the chance to catch up with mum, dad, brothers and sisters. They got their cuddles and loves.

Their return always followed the same routine. The lad, along with whoever brought him back to the home, would go into the *Super's* office. There they would talk for about 30 minutes before the group broke up. The parting would always be friendly, the social worker or policeman would be satisfied that they had got to the root of the problem, and all would be good. But by the time their car had reached the first cattle grid down the road, the *Super* would have the lad back in his office, shouting at the top of his voice and letting the boy know in no uncertain terms what would happen if he did it again.

Ongoing punishment took many forms. The runaway might have to stand outside the office door for several hours on a daily basis until the *Super* said otherwise. There was always the withholding of pocket money or a holiday fine. He might be told to complete any of the job rotas on his own, taking up all his spare time. It went without saying the lad was not allowed out to play for a minimum of a week, sometimes two. There was even one punishment where the *Super* forbade any of us lads to talk to the transgressor and likewise for him not to talk to any of us.

Running away was a very serious offence and would incur the wrath of the *Super*. But there was one *nicking off* that had an element of the Keystone Kops about it. It involved three of the younger lads - William and Michael, both eight-year-olds and 10-year-old Stephen. Michael and Stephen were brothers, the three of them had formed their own little gang and were inseparable.

There was an instance of one of the older boys in the home taking an unauthorised trip home. A trip that continued for over a week. Evading detection, he lived rough in and around the town where he lived, calling in on his mother at a whim and leaving just as fast. Apparently, the social services were aware he was in the town but could do nothing to detain him. His comedown was due to police intervention on the grounds of the council having a duty of care and the need to stop him living rough.

The lad was caught one evening when he again visited his mother and under the guidance of the social services, was brought back into care at *Hill Top*. The usual pantomime followed and during the following day as the tale of his freedom was told and re-told among the lads, he took on the mantle as a folk hero, a junior Robin Hood.

William, Michael and Stephen would sit and listen to his tales. Mouths dropping open, hanging on to his every word. It was hero worship in every sense. Stephen, being the older of the group, gathered his troops up on the lawn one Saturday morning after breakfast. The three of them had great ideas of being just like Robin Hood, living rough and avoiding being caught. They went down the far side of the lawn into a small coppice of trees and bushes. This area was out of bounds and we could only go there if a ball was kicked over the fence and then only to retrieve it and come straight back.

The three were discovered missing at lunch time that same day. The *Super* and staff looked all around the home, checking all four levels and all rooms. The search switched to outside. The older boys were mobilised into the search team with a brief to look in pairs.

Every inch of the grounds was searched, including the out of bounds areas, with not a sniff of the three youngsters. We called and called, and the search moved out onto the moor, directly behind the children's home.

We even had searchers up by White Wells and further over at the Cow and Calf rocks but still no sign. We were told to be back for teatime but no one had found the missing boys so the *Super* put the tried and tested protocol in place and phoned the police. They came in quick time, before we had finished our tea. *Super* took them into his office to give them a description and background to the lads then the two police officers did their own search of the grounds before heading off back into Ilkley to set the wheels in motion.

After tea, with kitchen duties done, we went back out to play football on the lawn. I picked my side and Stewart, one of the older boys picked his. A year younger, he was as tall as me and just as skinny. We both enjoyed that enviable position of knowing we were safe among our peers. No one would ever think of threatening either of us or bullying us and likewise, neither of us would never intimidate or bully any of the younger lads.

We did, however, look out for them at school. School was a daunting place for the youngsters at *Hill Top*. They would quite often be homesick and would cry and sulk. They were targets for any would-be bully, but our boys knew they would be safe in our company.

The ball was kicked towards the back of the lawn, very close to the high fence separating the playing area from the coppice. Stewart ran to get it. The ball is never considered out of play on the lawn unless it physically gets kicked out. As he turned to cross the ball, he stopped. He placed his foot on top of the ball, trapping it, then he signalled with the open palm of his hand for everyone to stop and cocked his head as if listening for something.

I couldn't hear anything, but Stewart looked straight at me and beckoned to me to come over. Telling the other lads to stay put, I ran across to Stewart – then I heard it. *"Stewart, Peter, we're here, help us."* It was unmistakably Stephen. His voice was coming from the trees on the other side of the fence.

Stewart led the way. There was a piece of the fence that could be pulled back to allow someone underneath to retrieve a lost ball. I followed Stewart into the coppice, calling as we went. Following their voices, we eventually found the three boys, they were very excited to see us.

We found them almost at the other side of the out of bounds area with all three of them almost at the top of a couple of the taller trees in the coppice. I would think they were about 15 to 20 feet off the ground. Stephen was holding back his tears but the other two, with the initial excitement of being found, were now into full blown crying mode.

Earlier that morning, they had run away and set up camp in the coppice. When they heard us all looking for them, they went deeper into the tree line and started to climb two trees, Stephen and Michael going up one and William up the other. They kept climbing and soon realised they couldn't get back down. No one was about, the search had switched to the moors and their cries fell on deaf ears – until Stewart spotted them in the last five minutes.

The great *nicking off* adventure was over. Between Stewart and myself, we managed to get the lads down and see them back to the lawn. The *Super* was waiting. Stewart and I managed to convince him that they had had no intention of running away, they had just got stuck and no one could hear them.

They did get into trouble though for going into the out of bounds area in the first place. It was a lesson learnt though as the three of them realised it wasn't glamorous being on the run.

Then there was another time when the *Super* lost it. It was a real black day at *Hill Top*. The younger brother of three, Christopher, was feeling very low and missing his mother badly. His older brother had also been at *Hill Top* but had left when he was 16, almost two years previously.

Christopher was being bullied. It didn't happen very often and never in the presence of others. By now, I had assumed the mantle of being the senior lad and with it came understanding. I knew how most of the lads were feeling and I also knew the various triggers that would elicit any one of several responses and I made it my duty to look out for them. I had developed an ongoing self-imposed responsibility. This was a major part of my time in care when my guilt, at times, was over-powering. I witnessed the younger lads being abused verbally and physically by the *Super*, and the staff doing nothing about it. For us, this was how it happened. It was expected. We had to endure it – didn't we? But it didn't mean it was right.

Christopher was the victim of a lone bully. He was caught at a low ebb. On his way to school one morning, he took off and headed home. He didn't make it the first night, so he chose to sleep rough. By the time he made it to his mother's house, the social worker had already called – and left. Christopher stayed with his mother for two days and each time the social worker called, he would hide upstairs. His mother was not for letting him go.

Eventually, the social workers arrived and found Christopher. On his return to the children's home, the usual situation developed. The social worker told the *Super* in his office that Christopher was very home sick and was being bullied and all he wanted was a bit of love, cuddles and comforting from his mother. The social worker left, Christopher was called into the office and the door was closed behind him.

The expected shouting started but was quickly followed by a new development - screaming. In the dining room, we could clearly hear Christopher screaming *"No, no please no, stop Super, stop…"* and the unmistakable sound of slapping and the odd dull thump. Christopher's voice was getting ever higher and more anxious, interspaced with gasps and groans.

The *Super's* voice was matching Christopher's but his was venomous, almost spitting the words out, *"Don't – you – ever – ever – ever run away from my home again."* I had a direct line of sight to the office door from where I sat in the dining room. All the lads were sat in silence, eyes darting around to each other in the room, shrugging their shoulders as if they were asking what the hell was going on.

Then it went quiet. All we could hear now was gentle sobbing.

The door opened about 10 minutes after it had first closed behind Christopher. He came out clutching his arms around his stomach, I assumed this was where the blows had landed. He was 10 years old. He was crying uncontrollably and hobbled, crouched over, his arms wrapped around himself. Tears were streaming down his face, his left eye was closed-up, swollen and red and a trickle of blood was running from his nose. He was sent straight to the bathroom and the *Super* followed.

The *Super* was well known for his physical intervention, a slap here, a push there, a thick ear, we were all used to this form of punishment, but this was different. This was new and unprecedented. I had never witnessed such a fierce attack on one of the boys before.

We ate our tea in complete silence. No one could quite believe or understand what had happened. You could have heard a pin drop. No one was allowed to see or talk to Christopher that night and the *Super* avoided everyone's eyes and that evening in the bathroom, not a word was spoken.

The following morning at breakfast, Christopher came down and took his seat at the table. It was clear he had a limp as he managed to get to his seat. His face was covered in bruises, the eye that was closed yesterday was now sealed shut tight, the flesh surrounding the eye swollen, purple and black.

The bruising spread down his cheek and was varying shades of yellow. The side of his face was swollen to the point he looked disfigured. The other eye was not much better. He could see out of it, but it was bloodshot and puffy to a high degree.

Christopher didn't talk to anybody, and he didn't go to school either. The *Super* wouldn't allow him out of the home until all signs of the beating were gone.

I have no idea of what was said between the *Super* and Christopher during the two weeks when we all went to school, and he didn't. Christopher never spoke of the reason for his absence at school as the *Super* would have done that for him by phoning the school and offering a fantasy of a story to explain his absence.

Several weeks later, Christopher came to me up on the lawn while we were playing football. I could see he wanted to tell me something, so we sat it out on the side lines. The pressure had caught up to him, he had bottled it all up inside and was ready to burst.

In floods of tears, he said *"I only wanted to see my mum; I didn't deserve what he did."* We sat there for what seemed like ages, he sobbing, me listening. I wanted to do so much more but what could I do against the might of the *Super*?

Chapter Ten
What Lies Ahead

With my last summer holiday behind me, I was being prepared for life on the outside. I would be leaving care in the next few weeks. It would have been a year sooner, but as I showed academic promise, I was allowed to stay on at school, enter the fifth year and take my exams.

I didn't set the world alight with my results but I did get a grade 1 in English, which pleased my mentor and friend, Miss Weatherall. This qualification stood me in good stead in later life as a freelance writer and photojournalist, a job that was to take me around the world… but I digress.

The first priority of the social services was to get me a place to live and a job, and this is where I met up again with Mr Watson. He would call to see me and go over a range of jobs he thought was suitable for me and then arrange an interview which we would both attend.

The stigma of being in care was still with me even at this stage in my development. At the start of the interview, Mr Watson would introduce me in this way, *"This is Peter Foster, Peter is currently in care through no fault of his own."* A great start to an interview I thought.

I remember one interview at a restaurant in Steeton, the Currergate. The gentleman I met was Mr Mallatesta. I only met him for a few minutes but still remember the name. I got the job and was to start in the kitchen with a view to becoming a silver service waiter but the best laid plans and all that scuppered my joining the Currergate staff.

An opening much closer to the home in Ilkley was advertised. Mr Watson asked if I would like to go for an informal interview at a hotel. The job carried a live-in position, and better still, I knew where it was. I had passed it every single time I went to school or took a trip into Ilkley. It was a position as kitchen porter and waiter in the Crescent House Hotel, Wells Road, Ilkley.

The hotel itself was a typical early 20th century town house built on three levels and was run by husband-and-wife team Terry and Janet Hislop. The Crescent House was less than a mile from the children's home and the owners were fully aware of it and indeed, would have seen myself and my friends on numerous occasions as we went to and from school.

As hotels go, it was a small, family business with just one other member of staff, the cleaner, and the interview was very informal. Mr Watson took a back seat after introducing me, whereas the other job interviewers asked questions directed at Mr Watson. Mr and Mrs Hislop spoke directly to me. I was shown around the hotel, including where my room would be, right at the top of the house. There were two bedrooms up there, one for myself and the other for the cleaner. There were other rooms which could have been bedrooms, but they were full of furniture and storage items.

The Crescent House Hotel where Peter secured his first job on leaving care

After an introduction to the hotel, we had coffee and biscuits in the kitchen. Mr Hislop was speaking directly to me saying how he was impressed by my school results and personal appearance and said there and then that he would like me to join his small team. As Mr Watson and I left to go back up the road to the home, I turned and offered my hand to Mr

Hislop, *"Thank you very much sir, I won't let you down,"* I said.

He smiled, as did Mrs Hislop, and said *"When you come and join us here, call me Terry,"* and almost in the same breath Mrs Hislop echoed *"And I'm Janet."* Mr Watson was extremely pleased at the outcome as it was like a double slice of luck for him, he didn't have to go the trouble of finding me a place to live.

It was official now. I was spending my last few days in the care system and for the most part I had behaved, I thought, very well. My discretions at worst were talking when I should have kept quiet, which had the effect of annoying the *Super* and the staff. On more than one occasion, the only way I could voice my disapproval was by fixing a cold stare in the direction of the perpetrator. This one act of defiance was a win-win situation for me as there was no retribution because I was doing nothing wrong and when the perpetrator broke their gaze with me, I knew my point had struck home.

There was one treat I was unaware of. Mr Watson had pulled a few strings back in his office and arrived to take me to Wakefield for a new set of clothes to help me on my way. When we arrived, it brought back memories from my first visit only this time, I enjoyed it much more.

"This is Peter," said Mr Watson to the manager in charge of the clothing store. *"In a few days he's going to be leaving care and starting out on his own so we need a full*

wardrobe please, and wherever possible can you make it new please, he deserves it."

That sentence made me feel good. I had had little praise in the last three years and only then from my cricket pals and Miss Weatherall. We left the store with loads of stuff, I didn't know if I would be able to get it all in the suitcase I had been given, but I managed.

With my time fast coming to an end, the other lads were feeling down. It was becoming clear to me now that most of them, particularly the younger ones, looked up to me as if I were a big brother. Stewart was staying on at school, just like I had. He was a good lad, and I knew he cared for the other lads and would help and stand up for them so I knew he would take over the mantle, if you like.

My last night in care was emotional. I hated the regime, I disliked the *Super* and *Matron* intensely, I hated the way we were paraded around whenever we went anywhere in a group. Yet I didn't want to leave and there was an emptiness in my stomach. It was so strange, I lay in bed, wide awake long after all the lights were out, the lads in my room all fast asleep making the odd, involuntary snorting, sniffing and gurgling sound with the odd squeaky fart thrown in for good measure. Apart from that, deafening silence.

I had been in the care of the local authority for almost three years. The day I had arrived was a distant memory as were the feelings I had for my

167

family. Except for that first visit from my grandmother and Kathleen just after I arrived, no one had been to see me, no birthday cards, no Christmas card or presents, I was preparing myself for the next chapter in my life.

I hadn't slept well at all. The light was streaming through the curtains when I raised my head to look at the clock 6.10am. The memory of that and every minute of that day is firmly etched in my consciousness.

I got up and went to the bathroom, a small luxury having it to myself. I had a strip wash, not hurrying this time but enjoying the privacy. That was something else I would have to get used to again. Washed and dressed in my new clothes, I stripped my bed as previously instructed by Miss Green. The sheets were placed at the bottom of the bed ready to be taken to the laundry room, the blankets folded and placed at the bottom of the bed. By this time the other lads had woken up, each of them raised up in bed supported by an elbow. *"Gonna miss you Pete,"* said one. *"Yep, no danger,"* said another.

I didn't answer. I was feeling shaky. I was afraid I would start crying in front of them because the reality of the situation was beginning to sink in now. I had slept my last night in care. Today was the day I was to start the rest of my life.

Miss Copeland was on the landing, getting the lads up when she came to our room. She saw I was already up, dressed and my bed was sorted. *"What's this?"* she said, *"Can't you wait to get away from us?"*

I didn't answer. I had never liked her. She had her clear favourites, her little gang. One of her tricks when she was smoking was to blow smoke directly into the mouths of her entourage, so they could get their nicotine fix. I didn't like her at all, and she knew it. Over the years I paid the price for my mild dissent in the form of extra duties, confinement to the home, fines and so on.

By now, my room mates were up and heading for the bathroom. I had already seen the *Super* make his way and thought to myself, never again. Never again will I suffer the indignity of being supervised whilst I washed or bathed. I went in the opposite direction, downstairs. I placed my suitcase by the front door.

I had spoken two days earlier to Mr Watson after we came back from Wakefield. He had said that as I was just going down the road to the hotel, I didn't need a lift. When he left that afternoon after our Wakefield trip, he shook my hand and wished me all the best saying he would come to see me and see how I was getting on. I never saw him again.

I was dressed as smartly as I had ever been at *Hill Top*. With my case waiting by the door, I sat in my place at the breakfast table. No one else was down yet. I wondered off a little down memory lane. Looking round the dining room, I remembered the young lad who had been presented with the same meal both at teatime and the following morning for breakfast; the pocket money parades; the cruel mickey taking from the *Super*, directed not only at me but just about all the lads over time. I could hear the cook downstairs getting breakfast ready, the noises coming up from below via the dumb waiter.

The breakfast cereals were already in place, as was the jug of milk on the table, *"Why not?"* I thought, *"What's the worst that can happen? Sod it."* I got my breakfast bowl and took two packets of cornflakes. Taking two packets wasn't allowed but I could not have cared less.

The room started to fill up with the lads, the staff appeared, and breakfast was underway. The first meal of the day was quiet, not much noise at all. Usually there were a few mutterings under the breath, spoken with the hope that the *Super* didn't hear, but this morning it was very quiet. It stayed that way until the pots were being cleared away and some of the lads went down for kitchen duty. There was still a couple of weeks of the holidays left, and until they went back to school, it was down to the kitchen after breakfast.

"Foster!" the unmistakable whine of *Super*'s voice, *"My office in 30 minutes."*

"Yes Super," I replied.

I was ready to go right there and then but 30 minutes wasn't too long for me to wait. After all, I had waited much longer, ever since I first arrived. My overriding wish now was to leave.

With time to kill, I wandered up to the lawn. Some of the lads were having a kick about but I kept my distance as I didn't want my shiny new shoes getting dirty and scuffed. When it was clear I wasn't joining in, the lads stopped playing as well and gathered around me, wishing me well and good luck.

My friend Stewart wasn't there. He was down in the kitchen, but I had already told him I would be away by the time he finished his duties. Saying my goodbyes on the lawn, I went to *Super's* office for the very last time.

Since getting up in the morning, well before anybody else, I had this empty feeling left over from the previous night but with it a feeling of personal emboldenment. This was it. I was leaving, my own future was in my hands.

As I left the lawn and walked back down to the home, a feeling of excitement overwhelmed me. I stopped for a moment to glance over at Sooty's cross. It was still tall and proud, *"Goodbye you old bugger,"* I said, then it really did hit me, *"Bloody hell, it's happening."* I could feel my legs shaking. Making my way forward, I regained my composure and the shaking stopped.

It was time to see the *Super*.

The *Super* was already in his office when I reached it. Knocking on the door, he told me to come in. *"Now then Foster, it's that time when you stand on your own two feet. We'll be sorry to see you go, you have been well behaved whilst you have been with us."* Even now, when it came for me to leave, never to return, there was no warmth or compassion in his voice. I remember thinking that my behaviour at the home wasn't down to him, it was down to my upbringing and my own principles.

He opened a cupboard and took out a cash box and counted out some notes and coins. He said it was pocket money I was owed plus my accrued holiday money and a lump sum from the council to help with my immediate future. He gave me the princely sum of £7/15 shillings (equivalent to about £120 in 2021). *"You don't need to worry about paying rent, your new job has it all included but don't think you can spend it silly; you need to learn to budget now and live to your means,"* he said. The first bit of real advice I had ever received from the *Super*.

Now I really needed to go. I was always uncomfortable in his company and one-to-one sessions in particular, would make me feel apprehensive. The *Super* opened the door just as *Matron* was coming in. *"All ready,"* she said. *"Look after yourself and behave,"* she added. Not the most heart-felt goodbye, and it was noticeable that the staff, Miss Green and Miss Copeland hadn't bothered to say goodbye, not that I expected them to.

As I bent to pick up my case and make for the front door, the *Super* stopped me with, *"No, no, no, the boys use the door through the cloakroom. You know that's always been the case. Off you go."*

I was never one to colour up easily and lose my temper but, in this instance, I could feel my anger rising. I gripped my case tighter and stood up, my back to both the *Super* and *Matron*. At my full height, I was a good eight inches taller than both of them, I stood over six feet by now and was in my 17th year.

Turning round, I fixed my gaze fully on the *Super*. I coldly and purposefully spoke to him, *"I came through that door three years ago, I'm leaving through it now."*

With that final remark, and no response from the *Super*, I turned the handle, opened the door and stepped out onto the front drive and walked around the house to the big metal gate by the roadside.

The iron gate closed behind me when I let it go. The clunk of the lever told me it was secure. For the last time, I turned right, just as I had done probably thousands of times before and walked the few yards to the cattle grid. To the right was the old Roman road that took you up to the moors, up and out of the Wharfe valley. On, up and over the hill to descend into the Aire valley and eventually down into my hometown of Keighley.

As much as I had wanted to in the past, I never took this option. It was a direct walking route to my hometown approximately eight miles away but there was no home there for me. Had there been, it's more

173

than likely I would have featured on the *nicked off* list on numerous occasions.

I stopped at the cattle grid, looking down at the beams of steel running length-wise across the road and the mass of rubbish that had collected below. I think I paused here for about 30 seconds. I thought about looking back one last time at the home that had given me so many memories of my later childhood, memories I badly wanted to erase. No, I was adamant, I was walking away from that part of my life and I wanted nothing more to do with *Hill Top*. The future belonged to me and I could please myself what path to take.

With this thought fresh in my mind, I stood tall and placed one foot on the steel beams of the cattle grid followed by another, then another until I was on Wells Road. It was downhill all the way from here.

Afterword

Peter reunited with his sister Kathleen and brother David

In the years that followed, Peter was reunited with his brother and sisters and settled into life in Keighley, living with Susan, her husband Hugh and nephew Mark.

Peter's father appeared briefly, stayed for several months, but then left again promising to return. But both Peter and Susan would never see their father again. He was still fighting his demons and addiction to drink right up to his death from throat cancer at a date unknown.

Peter married Edwina in 1979, and together they raised four wonderful children, two boys and twin girls.

The events of those traumatic four years of Peter's own childhood were never spoken about until 2019, when Peter decided to commit his story to paper.

Susan sadly died in 2020. Peter, Kathleen and David are still in contact and meet regularly.

Peter now reflects on almost 30 years of life as a photojournalist on assignments for the regional press and over 20 years of providing illustrated features for the national angling magazines. Would he change any of those 30 years? Not a single second! Would he change any of the childhood years? Absolutely!

About the Author

Peter Foster

Peter Foster was a Chief Photographer and regional photojournalist in Dumfries and Galloway in South West Scotland. He worked extensively for the *Galloway Gazette*, the *Carrick Gazette* and the county glossy magazine *Dumfries and Galloway Life*.

Some of Peter's more memorable assignments included trips to Canada, Cyprus and the Falkland Islands. Peter also contributed illustrated articles to the then market-leading national magazines for Sea

Angling including *Total Sea Fishing*, *Sea Angler* and *Improve Your Sea Fishing*.

Peter's love and passion for angling spans many decades and featured as an important escape mechanism during the dark years of his early life following the death of his mother.

Now retired and back home in his beloved Yorkshire, the time has never been better for Peter to put down on paper and recount those four turbulent years of his early teens when he was beaten and mentally abused by his extended family immediately following the suicide of his mother and how the care system let him down badly as he both witnessed physical and mental abuse at the hands of those charged with caring for him and others.

They were four years that shaped him, making him sit up and take notice of the injustices, the brutal beatings and ridicule that was rife in the care system of the 1960s.

Now for the first time, those experiences are brought out into the open.

This is Peter's true story. Every word is a true recollection of events that shaped his life. A few names have been changed to protect the innocent.

Picture Credits

Other books by Time is an Ocean Publications

The Hill - Songs and Poems of Darkness and Light
Another Hill - Songs and Poems of Love and Theft
Asian Voices
Asian Voices - the Director's Cut
Blood in the Cracks
Don't Look Down
Luminance - Words for a World Gone Wrong
Death in Grimsby
Bones
Hot Metal – Poems from the Print Room
Poets Don't Lie
Contacts
The Man's a Tart
Western Skies
Reality Cornflakes
A Moon Magnetized This Screeching Bird
The Arbitrary Fractals of an Oracle
Dissect My Fragile Brain
Sonnets
Spiced Dreams and Scented Schemes
Minotaur and Other Poems
An Alpine State of Mind
Blue Note Poems
Love Like a Rose
Under the Weight of Blue
Echoes and Stardust
Wet Socks and Dry Bones
In Pursuit of Dragonflies
An Escape to Stay
Maggie Stirs

Printed in Great Britain
by Amazon